# STANDARDS FOR EVALUATIONS OF EDUCATIONAL PROGRAMS, PROJECTS, AND MATERIALS

# STANDARDS FOR EVALUATIONS OF EDUCATIONAL PROGRAMS, PROJECTS, AND MATERIALS

## DEVELOPED BY THE JOINT COMMITTEE ON STANDARDS FOR EDUCATIONAL EVALUATION

**MCGRAW-HILL BOOK COMPANY**
New York  St. Louis  San Francisco  London  Paris  Tokyo  Toronto

Thomas Quinn and Michael Hennelly performed the final technical editing
of this book. Elliot Epstein finalized the design work and Thomas G.
Kowalczyk supervised the production. It was set in Electra by Bi-Comp.
Kingsport Press was the printer and binder.

*Library of Congress Cataloging in Publication Data*

Joint Committee on Standards for Educational Evaluation.
Standards for evaluations of educational programs, projects, and materials.

Includes bibliographical references and index. 1. Educational tests and
measurements—United States. 2. Education—United States—Evaluation.
I. Title.
LB3051.J57   1980        379.1'54        80-12192
ISBN 0-07-032725-4

1 2 3 4 5 6 7 8 9 KPKP 8 9 8 7 6 5 4 3 2 1

*Dedicated to* RALPH W. TYLER

The development of this book was supported by grants from Lilly Endowment, Inc., the National Institute of Education, the National Science Foundation, and the Weyerhaeuser Company Foundation. Additional support was provided by the organizations which appointed the members of the Joint Committee: American Association of School Administrators, American Educational Research Association, American Federation of Teachers, American Personnel and Guidance Association, American Psychological Association, Association for Supervision and Curriculum Development, Council for American Private Education, Education Commission of the States, National Association of Elementary School Principals, National Council on Measurement in Education, National Education Association, and National School Boards Association. It should be clear, however, that the Joint Committee on Standards for Educational Evaluation is solely responsible for the contents of this book. The formal endorsement of the sponsoring groups has not been sought or given.

Royalties from the sales of this book will be used to promote effective use of the *Standards* and to support ongoing review and revision activities.

# THE JOINT COMMITTEE

**Chair**

**Daniel L. Stufflebeam** (Western Michigan University), representing the National Council on Measurement in Education

**Committee Members**

**Henry M. Brickell** (Policy Studies in Education), representing the American Educational Research Association

**Donald T. Campbell** (Syracuse University), representing the American Psychological Association

**Ronald P. Carver** (University of Missouri—Kansas City), representing the National Council on Measurement in Education

**Esther E. Diamond** (Science Research Associates), representing the American Personnel and Guidance Association

**William J. Ellena** (Charlottesville Public Schools), representing the American Association of School Administrators

**Homer O. Elseroad** (Education Commission of the States), representing the Education Commission of the States

**Egon G. Guba** (Indiana University), representing the American Educational Research Association

**Philip Hosford** (New Mexico State University), representing the Association for Supervision and Curriculum Development

**Robert L. Linn** (University of Illinois at Urbana-Champaign), representing the American Psychological Association

**George F. Madaus** (Boston College), representing the National Council on Measurement in Education and Council for American Private Education

**William Mays, Jr.** (Michigan Elementary and Middle School Principal's Association), representing the National Association of Elementary School Principals

**Bernard McKenna** (National Education Association), representing the National Education Association

**James A. Mecklenburger** (National School Boards Association), representing the National School Boards Association

**Wendell Rivers** (Washington University—St. Louis), representing the American Psychological Association

**Lorrie Shepard** (University of Colorado), representing the American Educational Research Association

**James G. Ward** (American Federation of Teachers), representing the American Federation of Teachers

# THE SUPPORT GROUPS

**Project Officers**
The following persons reviewed proposals and reports and provided general administrative liaison between the funding agencies and the project:

**Daniel Antonoplos** National Institute of Education
**Mary Hall** Weyerhaeuser Company Foundation
**Conrad Katzenmeyer** National Science Foundation
**Ralph Lundgren** Lilly Endowment, Inc.

**Project Staff**
Staff members at the Western Michigan University Evaluation Center who wrote drafts of the *Standards*, coordinated its review and field testing, and carried out other daily project activities included:

**Mary Anne Bunda**
**Jeri M. Ridings**
**Robert J. Rodosky**
**James R. Sanders**
**Anthony J. Shinkfield**
**Daniel L. Stufflebeam** Director

**Panel of Writers**
Alternative versions of the initial statements of standards were written by:

**Marvin Alkin** University of California, Los Angeles
**Beverly Anderson** Northwest Regional Educational Laboratory
**J. Myron Atkin** University of Illinois at Urbana-Champaign
**Michael Caldwell** University of Virginia
**Carolyn Callahan** University of Virginia
**Nancy S. Cole** University of Pittsburgh
**Nolan Estes** University of Texas
**John Flanagan** American Institutes for Research in the Behavioral Sciences
**Howard Freeman** University of California, Los Angeles
**Gene V Glass** University of Colorado
**J. Thomas Hastings** University of Illinois at Urbana-Champaign
**Ernest House** University of Illinois at Urbana-Champaign
**Roosevelt Johnson** Federal City College
**Michael Kean** School District of Philadelphia, Pennsylvania

* Organizational affiliations noted were those at the time when work was performed.

**Stephen Klein** University of California, Los Angeles
**Richard Kunkel** St. Louis University
**Henry Levin** Stanford University
**Murray Levine** State University of New York at Buffalo
**Samuel Livingston** Educational Testing Service
**George Mayeske** United States Office of Education
**Jason Millman** Cornell University
**Laurence Nicholson** Harris Teachers College
**David Payne** University of Georgia
**W. James Popham** University of California, Los Angeles
**Ralph W. Tyler** Science Research Associates and Director Emeritus,
Center for the Advanced Study of the Behavioral Sciences
**James Wardrop** University of Illinois at Urbana-Champaign
**William Webster** Dallas, Texas, Independent School District
**Wayne Welch** University of Minnesota
**Blaine Worthen** Northwest Regional Educational Laboratory

### Consultants

Specialized project functions, including planning meetings, drafting
materials, editing manuscripts, and chairing small group work sessions
were performed by:

**David Adams** Western Michigan University
**Gilbert R. Austin** University of Maryland
**Robert L. Betz** Western Michigan University
**Henry M. Brickell** Policy Studies in Education
**Robert Carlson** University of Vermont
**Robert Consalvo** Heuristics, Inc.
**Homer O. Elseroad** Education Commission of the States
**Egon G. Guba** Indiana University
**Philip Hosford** New Mexico State University
**Robert L. Linn** University of Illinois at Urbana-Champaign
**William Mays, Jr.** Michigan Elementary and Middle School Principal's
Association
**George Madaus** Boston College
**Walter Marks** Montclair, New Jersey, Public Schools
**Bernard McKenna** National Education Association
**Diane Reinhard** University of Oregon
**David Rindskopf** Northwestern University
**Darrell K. Root** Lakota, Ohio, Public Schools
**Rodney Roth** Western Michigan University
**Michael Scriven** University of San Francisco

### Editorial Consultant

Editorial Assistance was provided by:

**Philip Denenfeld** Western Michigan University

**National Review
Panel**

The first draft of the *Standards* was critiqued by:

**Janice M. Baker** Rhode Island State Department of Education
**Robert F. Boruch** Northwestern University
**Patricia M. Bradanini** Solano Community College
**Ron Brandt** Lincoln, Nebraska, Public Schools
**Joseph Carol** Leominster, Massachusetts, Public Schools
**Rebecca E. Carroll** Baltimore, Maryland, City Public Schools
**William E. Coffman** University of Iowa
**Robert W. Consalvo** Heuristics, Inc.
**Wendy M. Cullar** Florida State Department of Education
**Richard D. Eisenhauer** Norris Elementary, Firth, Nebraska
**John A. Emrick** Stanford Research Institute
**Finis Engleman** Executive Secretary Emeritus, American Association
of School Administrators
**Gerald R. Firth** University of Georgia
**Marcia Guttentag** Harvard University
**Kenneth Hansen** University of Nebraska, Lincoln
**J. Thomas Hastings** University of Illinois at Urbana-Champaign
**Dale K. Hayes** University of Nebraska
**Ernest R. House** University of Illinois at Urbana-Champaign
**Madeline Hunter** University of California, Los Angeles
**James C. Impara** Virginia Polytechnic Institute and State University
**Edward F. Iwanicki** University of Connecticut
**James N. Jacobs** Cincinnati, Ohio, Public Schools
**David A. Jenness** Social Science Research Council
**Michael S. Kneale** Holdrege, Nebraska, Public Schools
**Mary Kay Kosa** National Education Association, Director for Michigan
**Barbara Lasser** University of California, Los Angeles
**Rose E. Martinez** Tempe, Arizona, Elementary School District No. 3
**Leslie S. May** Massachusetts Department of Education
**Alfonso Migliara, Jr.** Westbriar, Virginia, Elementary School
**Melvin R. Novick** University of Iowa
**Andrew C. Porter** Michigan State University
**Joseph S. Renzulli** University of Connecticut
**Patricia Smith** Worthington, Ohio, City Schools
**Richard E. Snow** Stanford University
**Jack Stenner** National Test Service
**Edwin F. Taylor** Education Development Center
**Nelle H. Taylor** National Education Association, Director for South
Carolina
**Charles L. Thomas** Research Triangle Institute
**Donald Thomas** Salt Lake City, Utah, Schools
**Carol K. Tittle** University of North Carolina

**Karen J. Uncapher** Alfred I. Dupont, Wilmington, Delaware, School District
**Beatrice Ward** Far West Laboratory

## Participants in the
## Field Test
The following individuals and groups applied the semifinal draft of the *Standards* to various evaluation tasks in field situations and reported their judgments and recommendations:

**Richard Amorose** Columbus, Ohio, Public Schools
**Carol Aslanian** The College Board
**Jackson J. Barnette** University of Virginia
**George Brain** Washington State University
**Alfreda Brown** CEMREL, Inc.
**Carole Clymer** New Mexico State University
**John H. Corbin** Kalamazoo Valley Community College
**Robert E. Endias** Western Michigan University
**Richard D. Frisbie** Community Mental Health Board, Lansing, Michigan
**Robert K. Gable** University of Connecticut
**Edward F. Iwanicki** University of Connecticut
**Michael H. Kean** School District of Philadelphia, Pennsylvania
**Sharon S. Koenings** CEMREL, Inc.
**Barbara Lasser** Southwest Regional Educational Laboratory
**William P. McDougall** Washington State University
**Jason Millman** Cornell University
**Alan Nowakowski** Bay City, Michigan, Public Schools
**Office of Evaluation Services** Lansing, Michigan, School District
**Ellice Oliver** The Wellington County Board of Education, Guelph, Ontario
**Timothy J. Pettibone** New Mexico State University
**D. C. Phillips** Stanford Evaluation Consortium
**Ann Porteus** Stanford Evaluation Consortium
**Jeffrey T. Resnick** Western Michigan University
**W. Todd Rogers** University of British Columbia
**James R. Sanders** Western Michigan University
**Carol Payne Smith** Western Michigan University
**Gary L. Wegenke** Lansing, Michigan, School District
**Blaine R. Worthen** Utah State University
**Elanna Yalow** Stanford Evaluation Consortium

## Participants in the
## National Hearings
The following persons contributed formal testimony in the National Hearings on the draft standards:

**Cordell Affeldt** Indiana State Teachers' Association

Gordon M. Ambach University of the State of New York
Fran Aversa Syracuse University
Robert D. Benton Iowa State Superintendent of Public Instruction
Jean Blatchford New Jersey Education Association
Carol Bloomquist University of California, Los Angeles
Mary Elaine Cadigan Guam Department of Education
Julian Carroll Governor of Kentucky
Jim Chrest Oregon House of Representatives
William Connolly Florida Department of Education
Robert Cope Kelvin Grove College, Australia
Linda Crelian University of California, Los Angeles
Joseph Cronin Illinois State Superintendent of Public Instruction
Walter Dick The Florida State University
Patrick Dunne University of California, Los Angeles
Elinor A. Elfner Wakulla County School Board, Florida
Novice Fawcett President Emeritus, The Ohio State University
G. Foster The Florida State University
Ray E. Foster Florida Department of Education
Luisito C. Fullante University of California, Los Angeles
Robert Gable University of Connecticut
Jean Gabler Woodhaven, Michigan, School District
Nancy O. Gentile Syracuse University
J. D. Giddens Oklahoma State Department of Education
J. Wade Gilley Office of the Governor of Virginia
William D. Grant Maryland Department of Education
Ben M. Harris University of Texas at Austin
Ruthann Heintschel Ohio Department of Education
Edward Iwanicki University of Connecticut
Randy L. Kimbrough Kentucky Department of Instruction
Michael Kirst California Sate Board of Education
David Krathwohl Syracuse University
Robert R. Lange Colorado State University
Charles Lotte University of California, Los Angeles
Kenneth C. Madden State Superintendent, Delaware
Robert J. Manley National Educational Leadership Services, Inc.
Billie Frances McClellan Palm Beach Atlantic College
Robert McClure National Education Association
Robert Morgado Secretary to the Governor of New York
Carl D. Novak Lincoln, Nebraska, Public Schools
Janet Pieter University of California, Los Angeles
Tjeerd Plomp Toegepaste Onderwijskunde, The Netherlands
Edward R. Savage American Council of Life Insurance
Lowell Simpson National Educational Leadership Services, Inc.
M. Herman Sims Ohio Department of Education
Carol Payne Smith Western Michigan University
David C. Smith University of Florida

**Robert Stake** University of Illinois at Urbana-Champaign
**Donald J. Steele** Toledo, Ohio, Public Schools
**Wayne Teague** Alabama Superintendent of Education
**Ralph G. Vedros** Florida Department of Education
**Robert A. Withey** Vermont Commissioner of Education
**Marda Woodbury** Research Ventures
**Toby Yager** Syracuse University

### Western Michigan University Student Assistants

The following persons contributed variously to the conduct of project activities through courses, donated services, and research assistantships:

**Kuriakose Athappilly**
**Craig Cameron**
**Randy E. Demaline**
**David J. Eaton**
**Phil Harrington**
**Muriel L. Katzenmeyer**
**Ronald A. Krol**
**Grant Lorenz**
**Lorraine A. Marcantonio**
**Alan Nowakowski**
**Wayne W. Petroelje**
**Thomas M. Reed**
**Laurence E. Rudolph**
**Eileen Stryker**
**James W. Sutherland**
**Robert I. Wells**

### Design Consultants

The concept and production of the design for the *Standards* respectively were provided by:

**Jani Mohr** Western Michigan University
**Debbie Anzick** Western Michigan University
**Elizabeth Westley** Western Michigan University

### Clerical Assistants

Most of the project's typing and clerical work was performed by:

**Patricia Burness**
**Klazina Johnston**
**Pam Sargent**
**Linda Standish**
**Jean Sullivan**
**Karen Wentland**

# CONTENTS

# FUNCTIONAL TABLE OF CONTENTS

## Reporting Evaluation

Most relevant standards:

## Staffing Evaluation

Most relevant standards:

# INVITATION TO USERS

*Standards for Evaluations of Educational Programs, Projects, and Materials* is the product of a pioneer project. The participants in it endeavored to develop standards that are both rigorous and useful. Nevertheless, the standards in this book are a first approximation. They must be tried, reviewed, and improved, as part of a continuing effort of many persons committed to advancing the practice of evaluation. To ensure that future revisions of the *Standards* reflect the experience and insight of users, we encourage those who use the *Standards* to send information about their experiences to the Joint Committee. To help in this process the Committee has prepared a package of information consisting of a letter of acknowledgment, information about the review and update process, and a supply of feedback forms with direction for their use. These forms request that the user:

a. Describe roles and responsibilities—e.g., those of the evaluator, client, and other audiences—that existed during the evaluation being reported;

b. Provide a summary explanation of the evaluation stressing application of the standards;

c. Provide copies of pertinent evaluation reports from the evaluation;

d. Note any problems in applying individual standards, as well as conflicts between standards;

e. Describe how any conflicts among the standards were resolved;

f. Identify limitations in individual standards and offer recommendations for refinement or revision; and

g. Identify areas not covered by the standards.

Moreover, the Joint Committee has developed the citation form shown in Appendix B which the user of the *Standards* may wish to attach to evaluation RFPs, designs, contracts, reports, and the like to which the *Standards* were applied.

Address all inquiries to:

The Joint Committee on Standards for Educational Evaluation
The Evaluation Center
College of Education
Western Michigan University
Kalamazoo, Michigan 49008

# ACKNOWLEDGMENTS

Many people and several organizations have contributed to the publication of this book. A number of these individuals and organizations are recognized in the opening pages; but, as Chairman of the Joint Committee and Project Director, I wish to add a few words of appreciation.

George Madaus developed the initial case for evaluation standards; and Christine McGuire and Willo White provided the impetus to get the project started and operating. William Russell was helpful throughout the project in providing it with an official organizational home. Daniel Antonopolos, Conrad Katzenmeyer, Mary Hall, and Ralph Lundgren ably executed their role as project officers in the funding agencies. Anthony Shinkfield was diligent and competent in synthesizing and compiling the first drafts of individual standards into a coherent initial draft of the *Standards*. Michael Scriven provided helpful reactions and suggestions on content, format, and presentation in the early developmental stages and served throughout the endeavor as a valuable advisor. Robert Betz made excellent recommendations to the project staff regarding how best to stimulate, guide, and coordinate this large team effort. Mary Anne Bunda conducted and reported on a thorough and instructive nationwide review of the first draft of the *Standards*. James Sanders coordinated an interdisciplinary review of the *Standards* and provided excellent advice and assistance throughout the project. Jeri Ridings maintained a history of the project, helped plan Joint Committee meetings, coordinated the national hearings on the *Standards*, and, in general, provided outstanding support to all aspects of the project. Robert Rodosky planned, conducted, and reported an extensive field test of the *Standards*. Philip Denenfeld provided invaluable editorial assistance; and David Rindskopf and Rodney Roth assisted ably in reviewing and improving the several manuscripts.

Beyond their regular role as members of the Joint Committee that developed this book, William Mays, Henry M. Brickell,

Homer O. Elseroad, Egon Guba, Philip Hosford, Robert L. Linn, George Madaus, and Bernard McKenna made special trips to the project location to perform various valuable functions. Extensive assistance was also received from the other members of the Joint Committee: Donald T. Campbell, Ronald P. Carver, Esther Diamond, William J. Ellena, James A. Mecklenburger, Wendell Rivers, Lorrie Shepard and James G. Ward.

Jani Mohr and Debbie Anzick provided creative and concrete assistance in designing and producing the format of the book. Klazina Johnson and Karen Wentland provided excellent clerical support throughout the project.

In addition to the persons named above, my thanks are extended to the many others who contributed to the *Standards*, especially those persons named in the opening pages.

Several organizations must also be acknowledged for their contributions to the Evaluation Standards Project. Lilly Endowment, Inc., The National Institute of Education, the National Science Foundation, and the Weyerhaeuser Company Foundation provided most of the funds necessary to implement the project. The American Educational Research Association provided an excellent organizational home for the project; Western Michigan University contributed considerable administrative support to the day-to-day project activities; and the American Psychological Association and Policy Studies in Education assisted substantially by duplicating and distributing semifinal drafts of the *Standards*. Finally, the following organizations that appointed the members of the Joint Committee and supported their efforts throughout the project deserve special recognition for their collaborative effort:

**American Association of School Administrators**

**American Educational Research Association**

**American Federation of Teachers**

**American Personnel and Guidance Association**

**American Psychological Association**

Association for Supervision and Curriculum Development

Council for American Private Education

Education Commission of the States

National Association of Elementary School Principals

National Council on Measurement in Education

National Education Association

National School Boards Association

The persons and organizations noted above are a powerful force for improving the practice of educational evaluation. I am honored to have played a role in coordinating their efforts to produce the *Standards*; and I thank them for their support throughout the project.

D.L.S.

# INTRODUCTION

This book is for the use of persons who commission, conduct, or employ the results of evaluations to improve education: teachers, administrators, evaluators, curriculum specialists, school board members, legislators, counselors, leaders of educational associations, parents, and others. It is for those who work in or are concerned about elementary, secondary, higher, or adult education; and it is intended for use in both private and public institutions. It is a guide to be used in evaluating educational programs, projects, and materials.

The book is not intended to apply to evaluations of institutions, professional personnel, or individual students. Nor is it meant to provide a set of detailed technical standards. It is not a replacement for textbooks in such technical areas as statistics, data processing, measurement, and report writing; however, it does speak to the responsible use of skills in these areas. It also provides a framework within which detailed technical standards could be developed.

The use of technical language is minimal, though some specialized terms had to be employed. To assist readers who may be unfamiliar with these terms, or their particular use, those that are most important in understanding this book are defined in the text. The definitions of these and other technical terms appear in the book's glossary.

The book identifies and elucidates 30 separate standards. They are presented in four groups that correspond to four main concerns about any evaluation—its utility, feasibility, propriety, and accuracy. Each standard is explained and clarified through a commentary which includes an overview of intent, guidelines for application, common pitfalls, caveats (or warnings against being overzealous in implementing the standard), and an illustration of the standard's application. In the Functional Table of Contents the standards are displayed according to major tasks in the conduct of an evaluation. A more detailed explanation of this book's organization is presented on page 13.

**The Standards in Historical Perspective**

Major reforms in education have consistently been accompanied by major reforms in methods of evaluation. In the 1930's, '40's, and '50's, the advances in evaluation were mainly in assessing student performance. Starting in the 1960's, however, there were, in addition, many developments related to the assessment of educational programs, projects, and materials.

The vast expansion of city school systems in the 1920's generated the need for structured school programs through which millions of students could move in an orderly fashion. Nationally standardized ability and achievement tests were created to evaluate the progress of these students.

The progressive education movement of the 1930's saw aggressive experimentation with new content, new methods, and new materials. New evaluation designs, approaches, and instruments were invented to appraise the achievements of students who participated in those innovations.

Tyler's now famous rationale for evaluation became prominent in the 1940's. Based on his experience in the Eight Year Study of the 1930's, Ralph W. Tyler proposed that educators should carefully define their objectives and gather the data needed to determine whether they had been achieved. This approach dominated the practice of educational evaluation during the 1940's and the 1950's, and it remains important today.

By the 1950's, the practice of standardized testing had reached massive proportions, and the professional organizations concerned with testing took steps to regulate the actions of their members. In 1954, a committee of the American Psychological Association prepared *Technical Recommendations for Psychological Tests and Diagnostic Techniques*.[1] In 1955, committees of the American Educational Research Association and the Na-

[1] American Psychological Association, *Technical Recommendations for Psychological Tests and Diagnostic Techniques* (Washington, D.C.: APA, 1954).

tional Council on Measurements Used in Education prepared *Technical Recommendations for Achievement Tests*.[2] These two documents provided the basis for the 1966 edition of the joint AERA/APA/NCME *Standards for Educational and Psychological Tests and Manuals*[3] and the 1974 revision[4] of that document.

The 1960's saw an outpouring of new programs and materials in mathematics, science, and foreign languages and the launching of an enormous number of new projects to provide equality of opportunity for all students, and to promote innovation. These programs and projects were accompanied by a requirement, especially from the Congress, that educators evaluate their work. As a result, educational evaluation was greatly expanded and diversified.

Those who demanded more evaluation in education wanted to know whether the new programs were:

1. focusing compensatory education on those students who had previously been neglected;

2. bringing about achievement gains in students being served;

3. responding to valid needs of students in both achievement and nonachievement areas;

4. being designed with consideration of sound theoretical and practical principles;

5. being operated competently and efficiently; and

6. producing new and better ways of educating students.

Federal, state, and local governments allocated millions of dollars each year to help evaluators address these questions. These funds spawned thousands of evaluations conducted in most

[2] American Educational Research Association and National Council on Measurements Used in Education, *Technical Recommendations for Achievement Tests* (Washington, D.C.: National Education Association, 1955).

[3] American Psychological Association, *Standards for Educational and Psychological Tests and Manuals* (Washington, D.C.: APA, 1966).

[4] American Psychological Association, *Standards for Educational and Psychological Tests* (Rev. Ed.) (Washington, D.C.: APA, 1974).

school districts—whether large or small, experienced or inexperienced in evaluation. Evaluators responded with diversified designs, more elaborate procedures, better instruments, increased services, and expanded training. A great deal of time, money, and effort went into the improvement of educational evaluation.

It soon became important to provide professional judgments on whether evaluation itself was being performed properly, whether it was improving programs, and in what ways it could be strengthened. The Congress became impatient with evaluators' apparent inability to determine whether multimillion dollar programs were helping to cure the educational ills of children. Groups producing evaluation reports, as well as those using such reports, needed a comprehensive, carefully developed, objective, and useful way of judging evaluation plans, processes, and results.

As one response to this need, the joint AERA/APA/NCME Committee on Test Standards, which had been assigned to develop the 1974 revision of the *Standards for Educational and Psychological Tests*, considered including in that document a section on program evaluation and the use of tests in the process. They decided, however, that such an effort was not within the scope of their revision task, and recommended that a new committee be appointed to address this issue. Thereafter, a planning committee appointed by the American Educational Research Association, the American Psychological Association, and the National Council on Measurement in Education studied the matter and recommended to their organizations that they launch a project to develop standards, not specifically for using tests in evaluation, but for educational evaluation generally. This recommendation was adopted by the three organizations. Subsequently, additional organizations were invited to join the effort. The ones accepting plus the original three organizations appointed the Joint Committee on Standards for Educational Evaluation. In the Fall of 1975, the Joint Committee began its work.

**Rationale** The Joint Committee was guided by the assumption that evaluation is an inevitable part of any human undertaking and by the belief that sound evaluation can promote the understanding and improvement of education, while faulty evaluation can impair it. The Committee was also guided by the belief that a set of professional standards could play a vital role in upgrading the practice of educational evaluation. Finally, the Committee members agreed at the outset of this project that no adequate standards for educational evaluation existed; therefore, they undertook to perform a needed service by developing and publishing such standards.

The Joint Committee foresaw several benefits from the development of sound standards: a common language to facilitate communication and collaboration in evaluation; a set of general rules for dealing with a variety of specific evaluation problems; a conceptual framework by which to study the often-confusing world of evaluation; a set of working definitions to guide research and development on the evaluation process; a public statement of the state of the art in educational evaluation; a basis for self-regulation and accountability by professional evaluators; and an aid to developing public credibility for the educational evaluation field. The possibility of obtaining these benefits seemed to the Committee well worth the investment of time and resources required to develop this book.

At the same time, the Joint Committee was mindful throughout the project that developing standards in any field can be a controversial practice. Risks commonly mentioned include: promoting a field that possibly is not needed; legitimating practices within the field that may be invalid and harmful; concentrating attention on matters of relatively little importance, while diverting attention from major issues; encouraging bad practices because they are not explicitly prohibited in the standards; and impeding innovation.

In assessing these risks, it was essential to recognize that evaluation is inevitable. People in all fields make choices, and it is inconceivable that they should do so without assessing the worth or merit of options. The crucial objective was to ensure that evaluations would be conducted effectively, fairly, and efficiently. Standards could help by defining good evaluation, by legitimating practices that are consistent with this definition, and by thwarting practices that are inconsistent with it.

The Joint Committee is convinced, based on its deliberations and extensive input from many people, that these Standards do encompass a valid and widely shared conception of evaluation and the conventional wisdom about its practice. But they also recognize that no set of standards should be enshrined as complete and adequate for all time. Instead, they should be applied in combination with pertinent laws, other relevant codes, and recent findings from research and development; and they should be revised periodically as more is learned about evaluation.

Regarding the *Standards'* influence on innovation, the Joint Committee believes that its widespread use will lead to a general upgrading of practice and to the development of better and more efficient ways of meeting the evaluation needs of education. The Committee strongly urges that the *Standards* be used to promote and not to stifle innovation, and that subsequent editions be revised to keep pace with developments in evaluation. Throughout this book the Committee has proposed concrete steps by which those engaged in educational evaluation can attend to and minimize the risks cited above.

Moreover, in recognition of the difficulty of setting sound, usable standards, the Joint Committee obtained the assistance of many persons in establishing and testing the standards before recommending their use. A project staff located at Western Michigan University coordinated project activities. A national panel of 29 evaluation experts helped draft the initial set of standards. Sixteen graduate students at Western Michigan University reviewed and assisted in revising the standards, and a national review panel of 42 educators and social scientists reviewed drafts of project reports. The *Standards* was field-tested by 23 evaluators and evaluation teams, and many people participated in national hearings on the *Standards*. All told, several hundred educators, social scientists, school officials, and others assisted in developing this book. (Appendix A describes the involvement of these various groups, whose contributions are gratefully acknowledged.)

**Focus of the Standards**
The standards do not encompass a particular view of what constitutes good education, nor do they present specific criteria by which to judge educational programs, projects, and materials. However, they do contain advice for dealing with these vital issues. In essence, evaluators are advised to gather information which is relevant to the questions posed by clients and other audiences and yet sufficient for assessing an object's effectiveness, costs, responses to societal needs, feasibility, and worth.

The Joint Committee attempted to recognize in the standards all types of studies used to evaluate educational materials, programs, and projects. These include internal and external, small and large, and informal and formal studies. They also include formative evaluations (evaluations designed to improve an object while it is still being developed) and summative evaluations (evaluations designed to present conclusions about the worth or merit of an object and to provide recommendations about whether it should be retained or eliminated).

In addition, the Joint Committee wrote standards that encourage the sound use of a variety of evaluation methods. These include: surveys of various reference groups, archival searches, observation of school practices, school profiles, jury trials for projects, case studies, advocacy teams to generate and assess competing plans, adversary and advocacy teams to expose the strengths and weaknesses of projects, testing programs, simulation studies, time series studies, checklists, the Delphi Technique, Modus Operandi Analysis, goal-free evaluation, secondary data analysis, and quasi-experimental designs.

The Joint Committee also constructed the standards so as to help evaluators identify and confront political realities. Particularly, the Committee sees information and money as two sources of power that may be used to corrupt evaluations. The standards, if followed, should help to ensure that evaluators and their clients will not misuse their power.

**Audience**   As noted earlier, the standards presented here are for the use of persons who commission, conduct, or employ the results of evaluations; and they apply to the entire range of tasks in an evaluation.

Teachers, counselors, curriculum specialists, leaders of educational organizations, psychologists, parents, students, administrators, school board members, and others involved with school districts should find the standards useful for meeting such responsibilities as judging or commenting on plans for school district evaluation and accountability systems, deciding whether to conduct an evaluation, judging external agencies' bids to evaluate particular school district programs, deciding whether to accept the findings and recommendations of given evaluation reports, designing and conducting their own evaluations, and playing supportive roles in evaluations.

Legislators and funding agency personnel should find guidance for planning the evaluation of legislative programs, writing requests for evaluation proposals, judging competing evaluation designs, and assessing evaluation reports.

Evaluators, directors of testing, and researchers should be aided in assessing the adequacy of their evaluation designs and reports, deciding what to teach in their evaluation training programs, and making informed decisions about what improvements are needed in evaluation methodology.

But these are simply examples. The Joint Committee rejects the narrow stereotype which pictures evaluations as being conducted by evaluation specialists and used by other educators and by lay citizens. The Committee believes, instead, that educators, psychologists, students, parents, school board members, legislators, and indeed the general public can be legitimately both the producers and the users of evaluation results. In fact, in the Committee's view, good evaluations ordinarily require the involvement of a team of people drawn from several of these categories.

Moreover, the Joint Committee does not believe that any particular evaluation task should automatically or permanently be assigned to a person because that individual occupies a particular position in the schools or in society. The Committee thinks that special tasks must be assigned to particular persons from time to time as an evaluation proceeds and that these assignments will differ from place to place and from circumstance to circumstance. Each of these individuals, of course, must have whatever training and experience are required to carry out the given tasks.

**Applying the Standards** The standards presented are not mechanical rules; they are guiding principles. They contain cautions and warnings against the past mistakes of evaluators, and identify practices generally agreed to be unacceptable. And they propose procedures established as effective and ethical. Frequently, two or more standards reflect conflicting principles; while such conflicts often are not resolvable, this book calls attention to them and provides some guidance for dealing with them. The standards should stimulate and aid those people who conduct and use evaluations, but successful evaluation requires that evaluators employ their own creativity, ingenuity, and good judgment.

Regardless of the nature of the evaluation under consideration, those concerned with it should reflect carefully on the standards and how they apply to specific situations, especially at key checkpoints in any evaluation process. These include:

1. deciding whether to evaluate;

2. defining the evaluation problem;

3. writing a contract to cover and control an evaluation;

4. designing an evaluation;

5. budgeting for an evaluation;

6. staffing an evaluation;

7. administering and monitoring evaluation operations;

8. producing and communicating evaluation reports;

9. evaluating an evaluation;

10. developing evaluation policies;

11. training evaluators; and

12. deciding what to do with evaluation results.

The importance of a standard at any one of these checkpoints depends upon the context of the evaluation. For example, the one that calls for a formal agreement to guide the evaluation is much more applicable to a large-scale, external, summative evaluation than it is to a small-scale, internal, formative evaluation. In the former type of situation a formal contract is often required; whereas in the latter type a memorandum of agreement usually is sufficient. Nevertheless, in varying ways and degrees, this standard and all the others are applicable in all situations.

A particular difficulty in applying the standards is that one or more of them will sometimes conflict with one or more of the others. For example, efforts to produce valid and reliable information may make it difficult to produce needed reports in time to have an impact on crucial decisions. Or, the attempt to keep an evaluation within cost limits may conflict directly with meeting such standards as Information Scope and Selection and Report Dissemination. Evaluators should recognize and deal as judiciously as they can with such conflicts.

Still another consideration in applying the standards is that they can be met only through a shared responsibility and commitment of all parties to the evaluation—evaluators, clients, those providing information, and other stakeholders involved in the evaluation.

Since the Joint Committee believes that the relative importance of individual standards will differ from situation to situation, it recommends that all standards be considered equally important until they can be ranked in the context of a particular situation. The persons considering doing an evaluation should reason together to perform this ranking, and should apply the standards accordingly.

If it appears likely that the evaluation will violate any standard judged to be important in the given situation, the evaluators should note what standards could not be met because of time, cost, or other constraints. If the violations seem likely to impair the evaluation so that its findings will be of little use or probably not worth the trouble and cost to get them, the evaluators should consider dropping the project. In general, evaluators should not avoid application of a standard because of insufficient time, budget, or client interest.

Whether a given standard has been met in a particular situation is, finally, a matter of judgment. The Committee does not believe that precise decision rules regarding the satisfaction of the standards should be prespecified. Such rules would be arbitrary and not universally applicable; they would likely delude and mislead.

However, evaluators who cite these standards should communicate clearly how they were used, what judgments about meeting the standards were reached, and what evidence exists to support the judgments (recommendations for applying and citing the standards are provided in Appendix B).

In presenting each standard, the Committee has illustrated common ways in which it might be violated and has suggested alternative procedures. In some cases, the suggested method for meeting the standard requires increased time and resources; in others the more effective procedure is actually less expensive. In the long run, the Committee believes that decisions to do only quality evaluations—even if this sometimes requires more resources—constitute a cost-beneficial policy for education. Sound evaluations can help improve education; poor ones can mislead those concerned with education, and discredit the process of evaluation.

Finally, the standards must not be allowed to stifle the creativity of evaluators or to impede the development of innovative approaches to evaluation. They should be used as a guide for assessing evaluation plans and reports and as a medium for exchanging information between evaluators and their audiences. Further, they should serve to identify needed improvements in evaluation methodology and as a base on which to build. However, the person new to the field of evaluation should view them as a necessary but not sufficient guide to evaluation, and not as a substitute for initiative, imagination, and training.

**Limitations**  The Joint Committee believes that this book expresses a valuable minimum general agreement about what principles should be observed in evaluating educational programs, projects, and materials. However, though the Committee sought and used the input of many experts in fields involved in evaluating education, the standards presented are, finally, a set of value claims that have been arrived at by a relatively small group.

The perception of this book as a necessary, imperfect beginning underscores the Committee's support for an ongoing project to review and revise the standards as evaluators gain experience with them and as they face unforeseen challenges. Only increased experience can determine, for example, how best to deal with tradeoffs between standards in given situations. Also, future projects to examine and revise the standards should consider whether they should be expanded. What is necessary now, however, is additional testing of this set of standards in actual field settings.

**Definitions**  To guide the development of the standards, the Joint Committee adopted certain definitions of key concepts. They defined the object of the evaluation as what one is looking at in an evaluation: a program, a project, or instructional materials. They defined evaluation as the systematic investigation of the worth or merit of some object. They defined standards as principles commonly agreed to by people engaged in the professional practice of evaluation for the measurement of the value or the quality of an evaluation. The Committee then defined program, project, and instructional materials evaluation as follows:

**Program evaluations**—evaluations that assess educational activities which provide services on a continuing basis and often involve curricular offerings. Some examples are evaluations of a school district's reading program, a state's special education program, or a university's continuing education program.

**Project evaluations**—evaluations that assess activities that are funded for a defined period of time to perform a specific task. Some examples are a three-day workshop on behavioral objectives, a two-year test development effort, or a three-year career education demonstration project. A key distinction between a program and a project is that the former is expected to continue for an indefinite period of time, whereas the latter is usually expected to be short-lived. Projects that become institutionalized in effect become programs.

**Materials evaluations**—evaluations that assess the merit or worth of content-related physical items, including books, curricular guides, films, tapes, and other tangible instructional products.

**Organization of the Standards**

In order to devise comprehensive standards, the Joint Committee identified four important attributes of an evaluation: *utility*, *feasibility*, *propriety*, and *accuracy*. The Committee is satisfied that standards which shape an evaluation so that it has these four characteristics are necessary and sufficient for sound evaluation in education.

Each standard in this book was developed to help define one of the four attributes. Several reviews of the standards revealed that a number of them applied to more than one attribute. Therefore, the Committee's grouping of the standards has been based on its judgment of each standard's main emphasis.

Utility, the first category, contains standards for guiding evaluations so that they will be informative, timely, and influential. These standards require evaluators to acquaint themselves with their audiences, ascertain the audiences' information needs, plan evaluations to respond to these needs, and report the relevant information clearly and when it is needed.

The standards included in this category are Audience Identification, Evaluator Credibility, Information Scope and Selection, Valuational Interpretation, Report Clarity, Report Dissemination, Report Timeliness, and Evaluation Impact.

Overall, the standards of Utility are concerned with whether an evaluation serves the practical information needs of a given audience.

Feasibility, the second category, contains standards which recognize that an educational evaluation usually must be conducted in a natural, as opposed to a laboratory, setting and that it consumes valuable resources. Thus, one concern is that the evaluation design be operable in the actual field setting in which it is to be applied, and another is that the evaluation not consume more materials and personnel time than necessary to achieve its purposes.

The three standards in this category are Practical Procedures, Political Viability, and Cost Effectiveness.

Overall, the Feasibility standards call for evaluations to be realistic, prudent, diplomatic, and frugal.

Propriety, the third category, contains standards which reflect the fact that educational evaluations affect many human beings in many ways. The standards in this group are intended to ensure that the rights of persons affected by an evaluation will be protected. Especially, the standards warn against unlawful, unscrupulous, unethical, and inept actions by those who produce evaluation results.

The eight standards dealing with Propriety are Formal Obligation, Conflict of Interest, Full and Frank Disclosure, Public's Right to Know, Rights of Human Subjects, Human Interactions, Balanced Reporting, and Fiscal Responsibility.

These standards require that those conducting evaluations learn about and adhere to laws concerning such matters as privacy, freedom of information, and the protection of human subjects. This group of standards charges those who conduct evaluations to respect the rights of others and to live up to the highest principles and ideals of their professional reference groups.

Taken as a group, the Propriety standards require that evaluations be conducted legally, ethically, and with due regard for the welfare of those involved in the evaluation, as well as those affected by the results.

Accuracy, the fourth category, includes those standards that determine whether an evaluation has produced sound information. The assessment of the object must be comprehensive; i.e., the evaluators should have considered as many of the object's identifiable features as practicable and should have gathered data on those particular features that were judged to be important for assessing the object's worth or merit. Moreover, the obtained information should be technically adequate; and the judgments rendered should be linked logically to the data.

The eleven standards placed in this category are Object Identification, Context Analysis, Defensible Information Sources, Described Purposes and Procedures, Valid Measurement, Reliable Measurement, Systematic Data Control, Analysis of Quantitative Information, Analysis of Qualitative Information, Justified Conclusions, and Objective Reporting.

This category includes those standards intended to ensure that an evaluation will reveal and convey accurate information about the features of the object being studied that determine its merit or worth. The overall rating of an evaluation against the eleven standards in this category gives a good idea of the evaluation's overall validity.

A review of the standards noted above suggests that some (e.g., Evaluation Impact and Valid Measurement) are relatively unique to evaluation, while others (e.g., Report Clarity, Conflict of Interest, and Human Interactions) are more general professional standards. This mix reflects the Joint Committee's belief that standards should be selected if they address persistent and important problems in evaluation, whether or not they are unique to evaluation.

**Format** The standards are presented in a common format to make them easy to read and to illuminate their interrelationships. The following format is used for each standard:

**Descriptor:** e.g., Context Analysis

**Standard:** a definition of the standard in the form of a "should" statement. For example, the Context Analysis standard is stated as follows: The context in which the program, project, or materials exist should be examined in enough detail so that the likely influences of the context on the object may be identified.

**Overview:** a conceptual/introductory statement that gives definitions of key terms in the standard and a general rationale for its use. This is an explication of the standard.

**Guidelines:** a list of procedural suggestions intended to help evaluators and their audiences to meet the requirements of the evaluation standard. These are strategies to avoid mistakes in applying the standard. The guidelines should not be considered exhaustive or mandatory; rather they are procedures to consider and to follow when the evaluator judges them to be potentially helpful and feasible.

**Pitfalls:** a list of not easily recognized difficulties that are believed to be associated with the particular standard. These are mistakes often made by evaluators who are inexperienced or unaware of the import and intent of the standard.

**Caveats:** a discussion of the tradeoffs that may be necessary in applying the standard in different situations. These are mistakes based on being overzealous in the application of the standard.

**Illustrative Case:** an illustration of how the standard might be applied, which includes the description of a certain setting, a situation in which the standard is not met, and a discussion of corrective actions that would result in the standard being met. The corrective actions that are discussed are only illustrative and are not intended to encompass all possible corrections. Usually, the illustrative cases are based on actual evaluations.

**Conclusion**    Taken as a whole, the 30 standards are a proposed working philosophy of evaluation. They define the Joint Committee's idea of what principles should guide and govern evaluation efforts, and they offer practical suggestions for observing these principles.

The Joint Committee urges teachers, administrators, professional evaluators, legislators, leaders of professional associations, counselors, curriculum specialists, school board members, and all others involved in evaluating education to begin applying the standards. The Committee encourages them to do so completely and diligently, to assess and report on the adequacy of the standards, and to involve themselves in improving the standards.

Under these conditions, the Committee is confident that the standards will lead to sound, useful, ethical, and cost effective evaluation services that will contribute significantly to the betterment of education.

# A
# UTILITY STANDARDS

## SUMMARY OF THE STANDARDS

### A  Utility Standards

The Utility Standards are intended to ensure that an evaluation will serve the practical information needs of given audiences. These standards are:

### A1  Audience Identification

Audiences involved in or affected by the evaluation should be identified, so that their needs can be addressed.

### A2  Evaluator Credibility

The persons conducting the evaluation should be both trustworthy and competent to perform the evaluation, so that their findings achieve maximum credibility and acceptance.

### A3  Information Scope and Selection

Information collected should be of such scope and selected in such ways as to address pertinent questions about the object of the evaluation and be responsive to the needs and interests of specified audiences.

### A4  Valuational Interpretation

The perspectives, procedures, and rationale used to interpret the findings should be carefully described, so that the bases for value judgments are clear.

### A5  Report Clarity

The evaluation report should describe the object being evaluated and its context, and the purposes, procedures, and findings of the evaluation, so that the audiences will readily understand what was done, why it was done, what information was obtained, what conclusions were drawn, and what recommendations were made.

### A6  Report Dissemination

Evaluation findings should be disseminated to clients and other right-to-know audiences, so that they can assess and use the findings.

### A7  Report Timeliness

Release of reports should be timely, so that audiences can best use the reported information.

### A8  Evaluation Impact

Evaluations should be planned and conducted in ways that encourage follow-through by members of the audiences.

# A1 AUDIENCE IDENTIFICATION

**Standard**    Audiences involved in or affected by the evaluation should be identified, so that their needs can be addressed.

**Overview**    Evaluations almost always involve multiple and diverse audiences. These include those persons who will use the evaluation to make decisions, such as boards and committees, individual administrators or legislators, instructional staffs, or the large group of consumers who purchase the goods and services being assessed. Other typical audiences would be the individuals and groups whose work is being studied, those who will be affected by the results, community organizations, or the general public.

It is crucial to identify audiences, to rank order them, and within resource and time limitations to strive to ascertain and accommodate their information needs. If this is not done, the evaluation may be a misguided, academic exercise whose results are ignored, criticized, or resisted because they do not address anyone's particular questions. On the other hand, an evaluation planned and conducted to meet the information needs of identified audiences is more likely to receive a positive response.

Criteria that are appropriate for ranking audiences include the expressed interest of each potential audience, as well as their prospects for using the evaluation to make or influence decisions.

**Guidelines**    A. Identify persons in leadership roles first, as they can aid an evaluator to choose other audiences.

B. Contact representatives of the identified audiences to learn how they view the evaluation's importance, how they would like to use its results, and what particular information would be useful.

C. Reach an understanding with the client concerning the relative importance of the potential audiences and the information they desire; and plan and implement the data collection and reporting activities accordingly.

D. Throughout the evaluation be alert to additional audiences that should be served, and, within the limits of time and resources, maintain some flexibility and capability to respond to their needs.

**Pitfall**   A. Making the evaluation too general by attempting to address the differing needs of divergent audiences in a single report.

**Caveats**   A. In tailoring supplemental reports for specific audiences, be careful not to distort the evaluation findings.

B. After identifying potential audiences, plan to accommodate their information needs as time and resources permit.

C. In contacting potential audiences be careful not to imply that all their information needs will be addressed; instead, help them to develop realistic expectations that take into account the methodological, financial, and political constraints on the evaluation.

**Illustrative Case**   A private evaluation firm was commissioned by a large state's department of education to conduct an independent evaluation of a major early childhood education program initiated in the state three years earlier on an expanding implementation schedule. During the preceding year, almost 24 million dollars had been spent on the program. The state school board had directed the department to secure an external evaluation of the extent to which the new program was "worth the money it's costing."

The evaluators spent much of their planning time by engaging in conversations with the state superintendent of schools, the department administrator in charge of the early childhood education program, and each of the members of the state school board. Without exception, those individuals were concerned with the cognitive progress of the children in the program— more specifically with their mathematics and reading achievement scores. Accordingly, the evaluators focused the bulk of their data-gathering efforts on securing first-rate indicators of pupil performance in math and reading. They devised a series of high-quality, criterion-referenced tests for each of these areas and gathered much performance data from pupils who were and those who were not involved in the program.

When the evaluators released their report, it became apparent that the state legislature, since it ultimately approved all fiscal allocations for such programs, was also interested in the report. Several key legislators, while attentive to the cognitive performance results, were far more concerned about the program's impact on students' attitudes toward school and their self-esteem. In addition, the legislators wanted a much more detailed elaboration of cost data than the report contained. Also, the report was criticized by early childhood interest groups, who viewed its contents as narrow in focus and, therefore, of limited usefulness.

**Analysis of the Case**  Beyond serving their client and their immediate audiences, the evaluators should have considered serving and accommodating a broader clientele. In planning their evaluation, they should have probed sufficiently to form some tentative conclusions about various groups' interests in the evaluation. They should have learned that key members of the legislature, such as the education committee of the state senate, and two strong advocacy groups favoring early childhood education—parents of participating children and paraprofessionals employed in the program—would be deeply interested in the results.

With that knowledge, the evaluators could have informed the state board of education that other audiences were interested in the final report and could have argued that their interests were legitimate and that their political action might be decisive in determining the consequences of the evaluation.

# A2 EVALUATOR CREDIBILITY

**Standard**  The persons conducting the evaluation should be both trustworthy and competent to perform the evaluation, so that their findings achieve maximum credibility and acceptance.

**Overview**  Evaluators are credible to the extent that they exhibit the training, technical competence, substantive knowledge, experience, integrity, public relations skills, and other characteristics considered necessary by the client and other users of the evaluation reports. Since few individuals possess all of the characteristics needed for particular evaluations, it is often necessary that an evaluation be done by a team of persons who collectively possess those qualifications.

Evaluators should establish their credibility with the client and other users at the outset of the evaluation. If the confidence and trust of these audiences cannot be secured, the evaluators should seriously consider not proceeding. For, if they go ahead when they are not considered qualified by their audiences, they may find later that their findings and recommendations—however technically adequate—are ignored or rejected.

In conducting an evaluation, evaluators should maintain a pattern of consistent, open, and continuing communication with their client. They should also keep in mind that the fundamental test of their credibility will rest in an ability to defend the technical adequacy, integrity, utility, and practicality of their reports.

**Guidelines**  A. Stay abreast of social and political forces associated with the evaluation, especially those linked to race and socioeconomic status (see D2, Context Analysis and B2, Political Viability).

B. Ensure that both the work plan and the composition of the evaluation team are responsive to the concerns of key audiences (see A1, Audience Identification and A3, Information Scope and Selection).

C. Consider having the evaluation plan reviewed and the evaluation work audited by another evaluator whose credentials are acceptable to the client.

D. Consider alternative evaluation procedures in the process of planning the evaluation (see D3, Described Purposes and Procedures).

E. Be clear in describing the evaluation plan to various audiences and demonstrate that the plan is realistic and technically sound.

F. Keep audiences informed about the progress of the evaluation through such means as newsletters, progress reports, memoranda, press releases, and meetings.

**Pitfalls**  A. Failing to establish the evaluator's credibility in both the substantive and methodological areas of the evaluation

B. Pursuing an evaluation biased towards the values of particular audiences at the expense of ignoring or minimizing other audiences' values

C. Failing to disqualify oneself for lack of the skills, experience, or breadth of perspective required to do an evaluation

D. Failing to ensure that the members of the evaluation team will devote time and effort, not just their reputations, to the evaluation

**Caveat**  A. Understand that resources are used up in efforts to achieve credibility and acceptance, so that too much emphasis on these factors results in lowered cost-effectiveness of the evaluation.

**Illustrative Case**  A school of law instituted a program for the tutoring of minority students admitted to the school but who had not scored well in measures traditionally used to screen applicants. School representatives worked with the university's Teaching/Learning Center to develop programmed materials which the minority students could use to improve their basic communication and study skills.

Two professors of law, themselves minority group members, felt the materials were inappropriate because they did not take account of the cultural barriers constraining the learning of minority students. They, therefore, undertook an evaluation of the materials, although neither had any prior evaluation training or experience. The evaluation report they produced was based almost entirely on anecdotal data drawn from interviews with a few students who volunteered to talk about their experiences in the Teaching/Learning Center.

The dean of the school, upon receiving their report, invited his department chairpersons and representatives of the Teaching/Learning Center to a meeting to discuss it. At the meeting they politely but firmly rejected the evaluators' recommendations. They agreed that the professors had been presumptuous in conducting the evaluation in view of their obvious incompetencies. Moreover, they felt that the evaluation was manipulated to confirm their personal biases. Finally, it seemed clear to them that the evaluation had not been commissioned by anyone in a legitimate position to do so. For all these reasons the evaluation lacked credibility; no one believed that a rigorous, independent investigation would have reached the same conclusions.

**Analysis of the Case**    Prospects for acceptance and use of the evaluation would have been enhanced if the evaluators had taken steps to ensure their credibility and the competence with which the evaluation was conducted. They should have sought the sanction of the dean, their law school colleagues, and the developers of the materials before moving ahead. They should have recognized the need for evaluation expertise to supplement their own knowledge of minority affairs (such expertise was available in the university's Teaching/Learning Center and the school of education). The expanded evaluation team probably would have planned and conducted the evaluation more rigorously, and the audiences would have been more receptive to considering and using the report. As an alternative to an expanded evaluation team, the professors could have asked their dean and the Teaching/Learning Center director to appoint a qualified evaluator to assess the evaluation plan and to audit the evaluation report.

# A3 INFORMATION SCOPE AND SELECTION

**Standard**    Information collected should be of such scope and selected in such ways as to address pertinent questions about the object of the evaluation and be responsive to the needs and interests of specified audiences.

**Overview**    To have the appropriate scope of information, evaluations need to be relevant to decision makers' objectives, important to significant audiences, and sufficiently comprehensive to support a judgment of worth and merit. Most evaluations are of concern to multiple audiences, each of which may have an opportunity to influence the evaluation design and have a claim for access to the results.

Each audience can be expected to raise a number of different issues concerning the object to be evaluated. From these, the evaluators must select those of greatest importance to central audiences and respond to them with information which is understandable and useful. But the evaluation should also assess the object in terms of all important variables (e.g., effectiveness, harmful side effects, costs, responses to societal needs, and feasibility) whether or not the audiences specifically ask for such information.

It will not be possible to gather all the information requested by all audiences. But not all information is equally important or essential to a sound evaluation. Once the potential body of information has been identified, however, it must be culled to eliminate what is minor and to emphasize the most important. This weeding-out procedure requires judgment. The evaluator should ascertain what the client considers significant but should also suggest significant areas the client may have overlooked. Also the evaluators should review pertinent literature, including previous evaluations, theoretical papers, and research reports to help identify and prioritize questions to be addressed.

Initial decisions may be made about classes of information. But, ultimately, a decision must be made about each single item of information. Gross judgments can be made during early conferences with the client, finer judgments when specific topics are chosen for measurement, and minute judgments when data collection instruments are being selected or created. The evaluator should return to the client and relevant audiences for confirmation that detailed plans and instruments for gathering data will highlight the significant information, place the less important in perspective, and eliminate the trivial.

Evaluators, like other professionals, bring their own preferences to the task of carrying out an evaluation. Some, for example, are most concerned about cost effectiveness. Some are interested in cognitive outcomes to the exclusion of others. Despite their personal preferences, however, evaluators should strive to answer all relevant questions about the object of the evaluation.

**Guidelines**     A. Interview representatives of major audiences to gain an understanding of their different and perhaps conflicting points of view and of the different audiences' information requirements (see A1, Audience Identification).

B. Ensure that the questions asked of the respondents are directly related to the purposes of the evaluation.

C. Avoid giving the audiences the impression that all their questions will be answered.

D. Allow flexibility for adding questions which may arise during the evaluation.

E. Have the client rank potential audiences in order of importance and work with representatives of each audience to rank topics in order of importance to that audience (see A1, Audience Identification).

F. Work with the client to collate the ordered topics from each audience; to remove items at the bottom of the list; and to add items which the evaluator believes to be important even though not requested.

G. Distribute the entire evaluation effort (instrument development, data collection, data analysis, interpretation, and reporting) over the final list of topics, placing most effort on high-ranked items.

**Pitfalls**  A. Failing to consider the level of technical sophistication of audiences when deciding what information should be collected and how it should be analyzed and reported

B. Neglecting to update information requirements through periodic contacts with the client

C. Collecting information because it is convenient (for example, because instruments already exist), rather than because it is necessary

D. Failing to consider the tradeoffs between comprehensiveness and selectivity at every stage of the evaluation: developing the plan; setting the budget; choosing the instruments; and collecting, analyzing, interpreting, and reporting information

**Caveats**  A. Recognize that comprehensiveness competes with selectivity (information scope vs. information selection), and consider that the way to compromise is to select the information the evaluator and the client jointly agree will be most important to the most important audiences.

B. Address the main purpose of the evaluation first, and pursue other interesting activities—such as research on evaluation, research on the subject at hand, and evaluation training—only if resources permit and if such ancillary activities are likely to contribute to improving the understanding and/or development of education and/or evaluation.

**Illustrative Case**  A school superintendent decided to evaluate the curriculum and organization of the district's junior high schools, and formed a panel of evaluators consisting of the elementary, junior high, and senior high school principals. They were requested to complete a written report for the superintendent within five weeks of commencing the evaluation.

The principals prepared the report for the superintendent based on their own knowledge and beliefs about the school system and its needs, supplemented by limited staff and student perceptions collected with a survey instrument. Included in the report were sections on academic achievement of local junior high school pupils, national trends in junior high school organization (stressing the advantages of the middle school concept), present and projected enrollments, gaps in the junior high school curriculum, and the physiological and social development of students in the junior high age group. The report recommended that the school system shift to a middle school organization, with grades 6, 7, and 8 in the middle schools, and grade 9 going to the senior high schools.

When the report was published, elementary and senior high parents were disturbed that specific concerns of theirs had not been addressed in the report. Elementary parents, especially, were upset about the prospect of loss of elementary school leadership provided by the sixth graders. For instance, many parents looked to sixth graders to escort younger children safely to and from school. Senior high parents were alarmed at the potential overcrowding with the addition of grade 9 students.

Representatives of both parent groups complained to the school board. The board itself was irritated because the report did not assess the cost implications of the suggested reorganization and did not assess the impact of other possible organizational changes. The board supported the parent groups. The middle school concept remained a pipe dream of the principals.

**Analysis of the Case**   The principals addressed a wide range of pertinent topics, especially considering the short time available to conduct their evaluation. However, they did not adequately address some of the most important questions.

They might have avoided this problem had they asked the superintendent for more time to check with key audiences before designing the evaluation. They might have sought opinions from teachers, students, parents, and school board members about the kinds of questions they wanted answered and then provided cogent responses to these questions in the evaluation report.

Later, when the middle school concept arose, the principals could have systematically explored the views of these audiences. Based on reports from other school districts, the evaluators also could have compared the advantages and disadvantages of the middle school concept with other forms of school organization.

The principals might have prepared two reports, assessing both the pros and cons of a middle school for grades 6, 7, and 8. One report written for the superintendent and board (the decision makers) could have outlined the educational, organizational, financial, and administrative ramifications of a reorganization. The other, for parents, could have focused on the educational advantages and disadvantages of the recommendations.

# A4 VALUATIONAL INTERPRETATION

**Standard**    The perspectives, procedures, and rationale used to interpret the findings should be carefully described, so that the bases for value judgments are clear.

**Overview**    Value is the root term in evaluation; and valuing—rating or scaling an object for its usefulness, importance, or general worth—is the fundamental task in many evaluations. At the heart of this task is the need to interpret the valuational significance of the information obtained in an evaluation. Such information—whether quantitative or qualitative, process or product, formative or summative—will be of little interest or use if it is not interpreted against some pertinent and defensible idea of what is good and what is bad.

However, making a valuational interpretation of the obtained information is a complex and controversial undertaking. Among the issues involved are deciding who will make the value judgments and determining the procedures they will use. Several possible responses to each of these issues are identified in the guidelines below. But it seems doubtful that any particular prescription for arriving at value judgments is consistently the best in all evaluative contexts.

The point of this standard is that evaluators and their clients should thoughtfully determine the approach to be followed in assigning values to the obtained information and should reveal and justify their chosen approach.

**Guidelines**    A. Consider alternative bases for interpreting findings: e.g., project objectives, procedural specifications, laws and regulations, institutional goals, democratic ideals, performance by a comparison group, assessed needs of a consumer group, expected performance of the sample group, and reported judgments by various reference groups.

B. Consider who will make valuational interpretations: e.g., the evaluators, the client, the various audiences, some regulatory group specifically charged with these tasks, or some combination of these.

C. Consider alternative techniques which might be used to assign value meanings to collected information: e.g., having different teams write advocacy reports; specifically charging the client and other audiences to make value interpretations; conducting a jury or administrative trial of the object of the investigation; seeking convergence through a Delphi study; or specifically charging the evaluator to arrive at a judgment of merit or worth.

**Pitfalls** A. Assuming that evaluations should be objective in the sense of being devoid of value judgment

B. Failing to determine what value perspectives (e.g., educational, social, economic, and scientific) the client and audiences perceive to be important in interpreting the results of the evaluation

C. Designing the data collection and analysis procedures without considering what criteria, such as performance by a comparison group, will be needed to interpret the findings

**Caveats** A. Do not concentrate so heavily on the problems related to assigning value meaning to the obtained information that insufficient time and effort can be devoted to collecting and analyzing the information needed to promote and support such value judgments.

B. Do not limit the effort to judge the merit or worth of an object to just those variables (e.g., cognitive achievement) which were projected in the initial evaluation plan if it becomes clear that additional variables (e.g., motivation) not provided for in the original evaluation plan are pertinent.

C. Acknowledge that decision rules often are arbitrary and, therefore, subject to debate.

**Illustrative Case** The curriculum department of an urban school district reached the conclusion that the apparently poor performance of black children on a battery of tests routinely administered within the system was related to the fact that instruction was based on standard English whereas the children in question spoke (and thought) in a nonstandard form of the language. Accordingly, the department decided to commission the development of new instructional materials based on the local nonstandard English which would, in effect, perform the same function for the black children that bilingual materials performed for speakers of other languages. The department set up a pilot project, Title I funded in the area of 5th and 6th grade language arts. If this pilot project were successful, similar developmental efforts would be initiated in other content areas.

The head of the curriculum department asked the district's evaluation unit to provide a team of formative evaluators to assist the development team in refining and improving the materials as they were being developed. While aware of the fact that multiple audiences were stakeholders in the proposed program, the evaluation team decided, since it had been asked to do a formative evaluation, to focus only on the development team's questions. Thus, the evaluators decided to fulfill their mission in two ways: (1) by submitting each unit to a panel of experts who would assess it on such criteria as faithfulness to the vocabulary and idioms of the local language pattern, the modernity of its concepts, its internal consistency, and its integration into the year-long curriculum package as projected; and (2) by assessing each unit through comparing the performance on an oral test of those children using the new materials with that of children using the conventional materials, as well as by interviewing the "experimental" children about their perceptions and reactions. The evaluation team made recommendations for refinements and improvements in each unit based on these findings.

When some four or five units had been initially developed and submitted to the formative evaluation procedure, the district superintendent, several board members, and the instructional supervisors began receiving letters and phone calls from parents and teachers who objected to the new approach. Some parents of black students felt their children were being reinforced in a socially dysfunctional language pattern that both stigmatized them and militated against getting good jobs. Some parents of white children felt their children were being penalized—that the curriculum was being "watered down" because some of the students were slow learners. Some teachers objected because they did not feel competent to teach using nonstandard language and did not want to invest the time and energy that would be necessary to learn the new ways.

The superintendent, responding to the pressures being felt, placed the whole issue on the board's agenda. The board, after devoting most of three meetings to the problem, decided to abort the new curriculum and to return to the older instructional pattern.

**Analysis of the Case**    The evaluation team made a serious error in assuming that the objectives of the curriculum department were the only values that needed to be taken into account in conducting the formative evaluation. The team should have realized that audiences and reference groups other than that department would surely render judgments in terms of their own values, about whether the project goals were justified in the first place, whether some unanticipated side effects were occurring, and whether the project could be implemented if found worthy. Prior identification of such audiences, solicitation of their concerns and issues, and explication of the implicit values on which these concerns and issues were based, would have been useful. Thus, the fear of the parents of black children that their children would only be further disadvantaged might have been explicitly examined through systematic observation of their developing language skills, teacher feedback on classroom language patterns, and the like. The fear of parents of white children that their children were being penalized could have been similarly explored. The concern of teachers that more time and energy would be required in retraining than they were prepared to invest might have been investigated through a pilot training exercise. Systematic feedback of such information to parents and teachers would likely have allayed their fears or made it evident that they were justified; either of these outcomes would have led to a more rational and considered course of action than what occurred through the enforced decision of the board in response to political pressures. Even if the proposed curriculum were found to be good from one perspective (e.g., the curriculum department's) and bad from another (e.g., the parents of black children), so that a consensual decision could not be made, the board would at least have been aware of the reaction it was inviting and the risks it was running in making any particular decision. Finally, the board would not have been forced to make a summative decision before even the formative evaluation data were in.

# A5 REPORT CLARITY

**Standard**  The evaluation report should describe the object being evaluated and its context, and the purposes, procedures, and findings of the evaluation, so that the audiences will readily understand what was done, why it was done, what information was obtained, what conclusions were drawn, and what recommendations were made.

**Overview**  Whatever the medium employed for reporting—writing, films, filmstrips, overhead transparencies, tapes, or oral presentations—clarity is essential for audience understanding, report credibility, and application. In this context clarity refers to explicit and unencumbered narrative, illustrations, and descriptions. It is also characterized by conciseness, logical development, well-defined technical terms, tabular or graphic representation, and relevant examples.

**Guidelines**  A. Attempt, when appropriate, to supplement a formal written report with other communication techniques—e.g., dialogue, forums, television, or public meetings (see A6, Report Dissemination).

B. Communicate regularly with key participants and audiences.

C. Address reports as directly as possible to the evaluation questions.

D. Provide sufficient contextual information to give meaning to the evaluation as a whole, thus providing a firm foundation for conclusions and recommendations (see D2, Context Analysis).

E. Define all technical terms within the context and focus of the evaluation and in consideration of the audience's technical and statistical sophistication.

F. Follow summary statements with full explication of problems, objectives, and questions (see A1, Audience Identification and A3, Information Scope and Selection).

G. Write simply and directly, but not simplistically.

H. Use examples to help the audience relate the findings to practical situations.

I. Invite a review of the report(s) by representatives of the audiences.

J. Help the audiences understand technical terms used in reports (e.g., internal and external validity, reliability, standard deviation, and homophyly) by providing a glossary, devising summary and technical reports, and/or providing training opportunities for these audiences.

**Pitfall**    A. Failing to assess and report in accordance with the audience's ability to use technical language

**Caveats**    A. Report various perceptions of the object being evaluated even if this introduces ambiguity, but point out such ambiguity (see A2, Evaluator Credibility).

B. Don't let the effort to achieve clarity result in a distortion of the findings.

**Illustrative Case**    A school board, having requested that the district evaluation unit provide an evaluation of changes needed to strengthen ten specified areas within the system, received a wordy 250-page report.

The report was riddled with ill-defined technical jargon and ambiguities. It dealt in vague generalities with particular aspects of the program that required revision. It was imprecise regarding the exact nature of the changes needed at different grade levels and with different kinds of students. Recommendations were so broad as to be almost truisms; e.g., "Teachers should devote more effort to the needs of individual students." The tables and figures could not be understood without frequent reference to preceding (and in some instances subsequent) sections of the text. The inclusion in the text of whole tests and related materials required the reader to skip numerous portions of the report in order to maintain continuity in the explanations of procedures and findings.

**Analysis of the Case**    The evaluators should have focused on their audience's questions and responded directly and clearly. The body of the evaluation report could have been divided into sections corresponding to the ten major issues that were investigated. Each section might have described an issue, its relevance to the program evaluated, the procedures for investigating the issue (including sample test items), the rationale for these procedures, the findings obtained, specific recommendations drawn from these findings, and an explicit rationale for the recommendations with respect to findings and outside sources of information. The report might have been preceded by an executive summary and followed by a series of appendices. Recommendations might have provided clear direction as to what specific actions could be taken and by whom, such as "reduce the number of supervised extracurricular activities in grades 4 through 6 from 25 to no more than 15 and use the savings in teacher time to . . ." The writing might have been more concise. Necessary technical terms could have been explained fully in the context of the evaluation report. Finally, a set of easily understood directions could have been provided for reading relevant portions of appended computer printouts.

In addition to the printed report, the evaluators might have made an oral presentation to the school board. They might have distributed a printed synopsis of the findings and given a short oral summary of the longer printed report. Subsequently, they might have opened the meeting to a question-and-answer period.

# A6 REPORT DISSEMINATION

**Standard**   Evaluation findings should be disseminated to clients and other right-to-know audiences, so that they can assess and use the findings.

**Overview**   Dissemination refers to the actions—such as written, oral, and audio-visual reporting—of evaluators and clients to communicate knowledge of the evaluation findings to all right-to-know audiences. A right-to-know audience is one that is entitled to be informed about the results of the evaluation for such reasons as the following:

1. They are the client; i.e., they commissioned the evaluation.

2. They are legally responsible for the object being evaluated.

3. They funded the object of the evaluation through taxes, gifts of money, or contributed time.

4. They supplied a substantial amount of data for the evaluation.

5. They are stakeholders of other types, e.g., developers of the program being evaluated, persons whose careers or professional status will be affected, parents, students, and representatives of the mass media.

It is crucial that the evaluators, in cooperation with the client, exert special effort to reach and inform all right-to-know audiences. The evaluation can have little impact if those persons who could use or support its results are not informed about them. In carrying out this function, the evaluators and their client will need to use reporting formats and approaches appropriate for the different audiences. Normally, these audiences will have different degrees of responsibility for, and interest in, the object being evaluated; and they will differ in ability to comprehend technical information.

Because evaluators must share with their client responsibility for dissemination, conflict can result over ultimate responsibility for this obligation. When this occurs, evaluators must bear in mind that they are responsible not only to the client, but also to other right-to-know audiences. If the client misrepresents the evaluation or withholds its findings from a right-to-know audience, the evaluator must take steps necessary to inform the audience.

**Guidelines**  A. Define at the outset and with the client's advice the right-to-know audiences.

B. Recommend to the client during the initial negotiation that all right-to-know audiences be provided access to the findings and recommendations, at least in summary form.

C. Recommend to the client during the initial negotiation that all right-to-know audiences be given ready access to the full report.

D. When feasible, arrange to have persons who are independent of clients and evaluators audit the quality of the evaluation reports and communicate their findings to the right-to-know audiences.

E. Have representatives of the key audiences suggest what findings and recommendations, in what reporting form, would be of interest and use to them (see A1, Audience Identification and A3, Information Scope and Selection).

F. Negotiate an agreement with clients at the outset on a dissemination plan, specifying audiences and detailing content, formats, and dates for reports to right-to-know audiences, including the mass media (see C1, Formal Obligation).

G. Negotiate an agreement with the client at the outset as to editorial control and who will release intermediate and final reports, but reserve the right to release information about illegal practices should such information be obtained (see C1, Formal Obligation).

H. Reach agreement with the client at the outset as to the uses and release of information that is identified with given persons (see C1, Formal Obligation).

I. Check draft reports as appropriate with representatives of the right-to-know audiences for clarity and factual accuracy.

J. Provide a summary of the full report if the full report is longer than expected, even if a summary was not called for in the original agreement.

K. In planning the dissemination of findings, consider a variety of methods such as executive summaries, printed reports, audio-visual presentations, hearings, sociodramas, conferences, and newspaper accounts.

L. Meet with persons who will prepare short versions of the findings (including the client's public information officer and representatives of the news media) to be certain that they understand the results. Offer to review their summarizations in writing or by telephone before publication.

M. Produce reports in a format that makes them easy for the client to reproduce quickly and inexpensively.

**Pitfall**  A. Directing the report to the client or sponsor while disregarding other right-to-know audiences.

**Caveats**  A. Take into account that it is often easier to help persons improve their performance if criticism of actions and materials for which they have been personally responsible is private.

B. Take whatever steps are required to ensure that information about illegal practices uncovered by the evaluation is released even at the risk of jeopardizing contractual agreements.

**Illustrative Case**  A faculty committee and the principal of a middle school developed materials to be used in role-playing activities aimed at improving school discipline. The materials were then tried out in half the school's social studies classes. Following a year of use, the faculty committee requested that the school system's evaluation office evaluate the usefulness of the materials to determine, first, if they needed revision, and, second, if they should be used in all social studies classes in the building.

The assistant director of evaluation interviewed teachers who had used the materials and students who had been exposed to them. Additionally, he distributed a questionnaire to the entire faculty to see whether they felt there had been any changes in school discipline. The evaluator prepared a report of the findings, highly favorable to the materials, which he delivered to and discussed with the building principal. The evaluation report suggested few changes in the materials and recommended their use the next year in all social studies classes in nearly original form.

When the word got out, strong protests came from three groups: the faculty committee responsible for the materials, the social studies teachers who used the materials, and other social studies teachers in the building. The committee disavowed the recommendations because the results of the evaluation they requested had not been shared with them. A large number of the social studies teachers who had used the materials contended that they should have been the first to receive the report and hear the discussion because they had conducted the trial of the materials as well as provided much of the data on which the evaluation was based. And social studies teachers who were destined to use the materials the second year complained that they were being asked to buy a "pig-in-a-poke"—no one had shared or discussed the evaluation report with them.

**Analysis of the Case**  The evaluator erred in not meeting earlier (when planning the evaluation) with the faculty committee and principal to develop a dissemination plan and identify right-to-know audiences. When the evaluation was completed, he should have provided copies to the teacher committee and discussed the findings with them. He should have made a report summary available to the entire school building faculty. And he should have at least suggested to the principal that the report and its findings be discussed with those social studies teachers who had used the material as well as those who were expected to try it out during the second year.

# A7 REPORT TIMELINESS

**Standard**  Release of reports should be timely, so that audiences can best use the reported information.

**Overview**  Reports are timely when they are delivered to each audience at a time when they can best use the reported information.

The potential value of reports that arrive after the occasion for their use is likely to be greatly diminished. The value of reports so late that they cause decisions to be delayed may be almost totally offset by the negative effects of the delay. And reports that are not used constitute a waste of the resources allocated to develop them.

**Guidelines**  A. In planning the evaluation, find out which major audiences intend to make decisions for which they want information and at what times (see A1, Audience Identification).

B. Plan backward in time, starting with the targeted delivery dates for the reports, and make realistic projections of what must be done to meet the deadlines, allowing sufficient time to meet unanticipated problems and to meet requests for interim reports.

C. Get experienced evaluators to review the timetable, and then revise it accordingly.

D. Identify alternative steps in case the evaluation activities are delayed and cannot be returned to schedule.

E. Throughout the evaluation, be alert and, within reasonable limits, responsive to audiences' changing timetables.

F. Keep the most critical information needs in mind throughout the work, so that they can be met even if less critical needs cannot.

**Pitfalls**  A. Promising completion dates without planning a detailed timetable and ensuring that resources are adequate to do the evaluation

B. Assuming without careful examination that some other individual or group—outside consultants, subcontractors, or the client—can complete their share of the work within their own time estimates

C. Failing to check progress at intermediate points and to inform the client about delays that may cause reports to be late

**Caveat** A. Consider tradeoffs in order to get reports completed on time. For example, use a smaller sample of the population, shorten interview forms, omit peripheral parts of the evaluation, or shorten the main body of the report. But do not sacrifice technical accuracy in order to meet a reporting deadline.

**Illustrative Case** A superintendent of a suburban school district hired an evaluator from a nearby university to evaluate a new teacher aide program for the elementary schools. The aides were lay citizens who underwent three weeks of training before entering the classrooms. For each week of training or work, aides received the minimum wage. Because the program was expensive, the school board wanted to evaluate the first year's results before renewing it.

The evaluator collected several kinds of data during the year: pupil attitudes, teacher attitudes, aide activities, and job satisfaction. However, the evaluator spent so much time processing and analyzing the data that the report was not finished at the previously agreed upon time. When the board held its final summer meeting to vote on contracts with the aides it had to rely on the superintendent's undocumented impressions of program success in making its decision.

**Analysis of the Case** In the spring of the year, the evaluator should have reexamined the data processing and data analysis timetable, taking into account how many weeks would be available between the last date of data collection and the date the school board would meet to vote. When it became apparent that all the data could not be processed and analyzed as originally intended, the evaluator should have met with the superintendent, determined which analyses would be most important in guiding the school board's upcoming decision, and finished those analyses.

The final report should have been transmitted to the superintendent at least one full week in advance of the final school board meeting to allow time for careful study before the vote.

# A8 EVALUATION IMPACT

**Standard**  Evaluations should be planned and conducted in ways that encourage follow-through by members of the audiences.

**Overview**  The impact of an evaluation refers to the influence it has on the decisions and actions of members of the audience. A beneficial impact is one that helps educators carry out their responsibilities and, in general, meet the educational needs of their students. The thrust of this standard is that evaluators should help their audiences use the evaluation findings in taking such beneficial actions as improving programs, projects, or materials; selecting more cost-beneficial products or approaches; or stopping wasteful, unproductive efforts.

Evaluators must not assume that improvements will occur automatically once the evaluation report is completed. Such improvements must be stimulated and guided, and evaluators can and should perform an important role in this process. In effect, they should play the role of a change agent, i.e., someone who plans, staffs, and conducts evaluation activities so as to ensure that the members of the audience will assess and make constructive use of the results of an evaluation.

**Guidelines**  A. Demonstrate to key audiences at the beginning of the evaluation how the findings might be useful for their work.

B. Arrange for the involvement of representatives of the audiences in determining the questions and planning and implementing the procedures of the evaluation (see A1, Audience Identification).

C. Be open, frank, and concrete in reporting to audiences and be available and willing to assist in clarifying the reports (see A5, Report Clarity and C3, Full and Frank Disclosure).

D. Periodically report interim results, noting especially how these may apply to roles performed by members of the audiences (see A6, Report Dissemination).

E. Assess the merits of plausible alternative courses of action and discuss those in the final report.

F. Supplement written reports with ongoing oral communication (see A6, Report Dissemination).

G. Within limits of time and resources, plan to help the audiences assess, interpret, and apply the evaluation findings beyond the time when the final report is submitted.

**Pitfalls**  A. Losing interest in the evaluation as soon as the final report is delivered

B. Exhibiting a lack of confidence that the audiences will make practical use of the evaluation findings (e.g., by commenting publicly that audiences will only believe those parts of the evaluation that reinforce their current beliefs and practices)

C. Becoming preoccupied with the theoretical value of the findings at the expense of the importance of their application

D. Failing to consider the values of the audiences when making recommendations

**Caveats**  A. Do not try to assume the client's responsibilities for acting on findings of the evaluation.

B. Consider that many evaluators are not trained to be change agents and that they need specialized assistance to be effective in that role.

C. Consider actions that the audiences are contemplating based on the evaluation findings, and inform them of possible misapplications of the findings.

D. Avoid being influenced by powerful audiences to support recommendations which are not justified by the findings.

**Illustrative Case**  Through a state-supported project designed to increase parent involvement in an elementary school, a group of parents developed a guide and supplementary materials designed to assist parents of elementary school children to help their children improve their reading skills. The parents' group decided that the guide and materials should be evaluated and probably revised before being put into general use. Accordingly, they engaged the district's reading specialist to undertake the evaluation.

The resulting evaluation report assessed the guide and materials in relation to: appropriateness and completeness of content, format, readability, general ease of use, and effectiveness under trial conditions. The concluding section of the report identified weaknesses and presented recommendations for rewriting the guide and adding a daily progress chart.

The parents' group was pleased with the constructive posture of the evaluation report and invited its author to meet with them to discuss its contents. The reading specialist readily agreed and attended the group's next meeting.

At the meeting the reading specialist explained the evaluation report in great detail. She also distributed a new version of the guide and a sample progress report which she had prepared. The parents' group expressed gratitude for the evaluation efforts, and said they felt embarrassed that their initial products were so imperfect compared to those developed by the evaluator. They said they now realized that they were not capable of completing the task they had set for themselves. They convinced the evaluator to take over their role in the project and subsequently phased out their participation. The reading specialist finalized the guide and materials, but, to her surprise and disappointment, found that the parents of students in the school did not adopt and use the materials.

**Analysis of the Case**   The evaluator erred by being overzealous in assisting the parents to use the results of the evaluation. While her willingness to provide some follow-through assistance was appropriate, she should not have taken over the parents' role in developing the guide and materials—especially since the purpose of the given project was to increase parent involvement. She might have at least delayed her direct participation in rewriting the materials and, instead, have volunteered to review subsequent drafts developed by the parents.

# B
# FEASIBILITY STANDARDS

## SUMMARY OF THE STANDARDS

### B  Feasibility Standards

The Feasibility Standards are intended to ensure that an evaluation will be realistic, prudent, diplomatic, and frugal; they are:

### B1  Practical Procedures

The evaluation procedures should be practical, so that disruption is kept to a minimum, and that needed information can be obtained.

### B2  Political Viability

The evaluation should be planned and conducted with anticipation of the different positions of various interest groups, so that their cooperation may be obtained, and so that possible attempts by any of these groups to curtail evaluation operations or to bias or misapply the results can be averted or counteracted.

### B3  Cost Effectiveness

The evaluation should produce information of sufficient value to justify the resources expended.

# B1 PRACTICAL PROCEDURES

**Standard**  The evaluation procedures should be practical, so that disruption is kept to a minimum, and that needed information can be obtained.

**Overview**  Evaluation procedures are the particular actions taken in the process of collecting and using information to judge the worth or merit of an object. These procedures include, but are not limited to, how contractual agreements with the client are reached; how data sources are chosen; which instruments are selected and how they are administered; how data are collected, recorded, stored, and retrieved; how data are analyzed; and how findings are reported. The thrust of this standard is that evaluators should choose and implement procedures that minimize disruption to the educational processes being evaluated and that are feasible and realistic given the constraints of time, budget, staff, and availability of participants and data.

If evaluators do not adhere to this standard they may plan procedures that are theoretically sound but unworkable. Such a practice consumes resources without yielding valuable and/or usable results.

**Guidelines**  A. Choose procedures which can be carried out with reasonable effort.

B. Select procedures in light of known time constraints and participants' availability.

C. Check with participants about the practicability of the data collection schedule and various data collection techniques before finalizing the data collection plan (see D3, Described Purposes and Procedures).

D. Project alternative procedures in anticipation of potential problems.

E. Ensure the availability of sufficient trained personnel to complete the evaluation as proposed.

F. When it is possible, try out procedures and instruments to determine their practicality and time requirements.

G. Check with participants about the practicality of the sampling plan.

**Pitfall** A. Choosing a data collection and analysis plan from a research methods textbook or other general guide without considering whether the plan can be carried out in the given setting

**Caveat** A. Weigh practicality against accuracy. If circumstances will inhibit the collection of valid and reliable data, work with the client to remove or alter these circumstances. If this proves unsuccessful, seriously consider not doing the evaluation.

**Illustrative Case** A state education department issued a request for proposals to evaluate a state-supported school aid program. This program was operating in 100 school districts in the state and provided about $100 per pupil to schools with high concentrations of economically disadvantaged students. It was due to be applied in an additional 100 districts, and the officials of the state agency wanted to control the expansion in such a way that the effects of the program could be ascertained. Accordingly, the request for proposals specified that the next 100 program grants to school districts would be made in accordance with the requirements of the selected evaluation plan.

The evaluation proposal chosen specified that the state department should recruit 10 urban, 15 suburban, and 25 rural districts, dispersed geographically throughout the state, to participate in the evaluation. Each district was to be chosen only if its superintendent agreed to cooperate fully with the evaluators and to meet the requirements of their evaluation plan. Specifically, the superintendents were to do the following: identify two of their elementary schools matched for their concentrations of disadvantaged students and for similarity of program offerings; allow the evaluators to choose one of these schools at random to receive the financial aid; use this aid to enrich the programs of the disadvantaged students in the chosen school; and ensure that both schools would comply with the evaluators' data collection requests. The evaluation plan specified that the students in all 100 schools would be pre-tested and post-tested during each of three years, and that the results would be analyzed to determine whether the students in the 50 schools receiving the state aid achieved higher test scores than did the students in the other 50 schools.

The state department successfully recruited 50 districts that met the sampling requirements and whose superintendents agreed to the conditions specified in the evaluation plan. A grant was made to each school randomly chosen from the 50 matched pairs; and the evaluation was launched with the pre-testing of all students in all 100 schools.

By the time the evaluators administered the post-test at the end of the first project year, they realized that their evaluation had been hopelessly compromised. The superintendents had lived up to the letter but not the spirit of their bargain with the state department; for, in the face of possible criticism from the constituents and staff of schools in their district that were not benefiting from the new state grant, the superintendents had reallocated other discretionary monies so that no school was in a financially advantageous position. The result was that the difference between total per-pupil expenditures for the schools in each matched pair was negligible. Also, it was discovered that by the time of the post-test, student populations in the schools were considerably changed. There were many new students in each school, while many others had left. Also, in several instances students starting out in one school of a matched pair had transferred to the other. Because so many assumptions of the original evaluation plan had been compromised, the state department officials and the evaluators agreed that a case study approach should be substituted for the originally planned comparative analysis. Ironically, the state department had previously rejected several proposals that recommended a case study approach.

**Analysis of the Case** The evaluators should have known that giving preferential treatment to one school in a district was likely to generate political pressure to equalize the treatment across all the schools. Moreover, the evaluators should have anticipated student attrition and mobility. Accordingly, they might have considered with the state department whether data should have been gathered and analyzed at the district rather than the school level. If the state department insisted on a randomized comparative evaluation so that the effects of state categorical aid might be assessed in a relatively unequivocal manner, a randomized subset of school districts from a preselected sample of districts might have been chosen to receive the state grants. Then samples of students from each district in the total sample could have been tested periodically throughout the duration of the evaluation, and scores from the districts receiving the grants could have been compared to scores from the districts that received no grants. Otherwise, a case study might have been the more practical approach.

# B2 POLITICAL VIABILITY

**Standard**   The evaluation should be planned and conducted with anticipation of the different positions of various interest groups, so that their cooperation may be obtained, and so that possible attempts by any of these groups to curtail evaluation operations or to bias or misapply the results can be averted or counteracted.

**Overview**   An interest group is any group of individuals that seeks to influence policy in favor of some shared goal or concern. An evaluation has political implications to the extent that it leads to decisions concerning reallocation of resources and influence. Evaluations are politically viable to the extent that their purposes can be achieved despite the pressures and actions applied by various interest groups.

If evaluators do not institute measures to ensure that their work is politically viable, they will often find that their efforts are either ineffectual or misapplied. They may have to abort evaluations when they discover their work is being manipulated beyond their control. Or they may discover too late that their work has been used by one group to gain an unfair advantage over another. And they may find that their efforts can be stopped or seriously impeded by a group that is threatened by an evaluation. On the positive side, evaluators who are sensitive to political pressures often will be able to make constructive use of diverse political forces in achieving the purposes of the evaluation.

**Guidelines**   A. Before agreeing to do a potentially volatile evaluation, meet with as many interest groups as possible, give them an opportunity to express their positions and concerns regarding the evaluation, and assure them that it will be conducted on an impartial basis (see A8, Evaluation Impact and D3, Described Purposes and Procedures).

B. Negotiate a contract which makes explicit and public the conditions that will govern the evaluation and which assures that evaluators will have access to the required data and control over the editing and dissemination of their reports (see C1, Formal Obligation).

C. Provide clients with periodic reports on the progress of the evaluation—through such means as advisory panels and newsletters—in order to ensure that reported outcomes of the evaluation are not total surprises to the audiences and that their reactions to the reports are not unanticipated by the evaluators (see A2, Evaluator Credibility and A8, Evaluation Impact).

D. Within available resources, identify, assess, and report the opposing positions of different interest groups.

E. Discontinue the evaluation if political conflicts are of such magnitude and create such an unfavorable situation that it appears the interests of all concerned will be best served by withdrawal.

**Pitfalls**    A. Giving the appearance—by such actions as reporting to some special interest groups but not to others or associating more with one audience than another—that the evaluation is biased in favor of one group

B. Failing to assess accurately the formal and informal organizational and power structure

**Caveat**    A. Avoid so insulating the evaluation from the possible influence of special interest groups that key audiences are not consulted and/or provided timely feedback that addresses their particular questions (see A1, Audience Identification).

**Illustrative Case**    A group of evaluators accepted an assignment in a school district to evaluate an innovative team-teaching approach to reading instruction. The evaluation was mandated as part of the state funding program which led to the program's installation. There were rumors that the district superintendent was opposed to the program because, although there would be fewer federal funds available if it were not in operation, these funds could be used with greater flexibility. Some teachers said the superintendent would do anything to scrap the program, even influence the evaluation so that it reflected adversely on the team-teaching program.

As the evaluators planned their project, they built in a scheme to assess individual teachers' instructional skills. To their consternation, however, when the design was released it brought an immediate repudiation from the teachers' union, which was opposed to the scheme for appraising its members. A strike was threatened if the evaluation was carried out as planned. The incident made page one of the local newspaper and received much attention on local radio stations. Fearing the consequences, the evaluators backed down on their demands for teacher evaluation, even though they thought such an action would substantially reduce the evaluation's defensibility.

At the conclusion of the evaluation, to the evaluators' surprise, pupil achievement data and other factors indicated that the new program was a clear success. But, when the superintendent got a preview copy of the report, he issued a public statement to the newspapers isolating a number of alleged methodological deficiencies in the evaluation, repudiating its conclusion, and castigating the evaluators for incompetence. In particular, he stressed the omission of the assessment of individual teachers' instructional skills.

The evaluators concluded that their project had been doomed to fail.

**Analysis of the Case**  Sensing the superintendent's bias in the matter, the evaluators might have developed a written evaluation plan and obliged him to approve the plan in writing or to suggest revisions so that it would be acceptable. By securing the superintendent's approval of their methodology the evaluators could have precluded subsequent dismissal of findings because of methodological defects.

With respect to the teacher-appraisal part of their design, the evaluators should have involved teacher union officials early in their planning, so that, sensitized to the union's views, they could have evolved a scheme whereby teacher evaluation data were recorded anonymously. Thus, no one would have known which evaluations belonged to which teachers. In addition, the evaluators and union officials might have devised an "informed consent" document which could have explained the purpose of the evaluation to each teacher, including the provision for the teacher's written consent before the teacher was involved in the evaluation.

# B3 COST EFFECTIVENESS

**Standard**    The evaluation should produce information of sufficient value to justify the resources expended.

**Overview**    An evaluation is cost effective if its benefits equal or exceed its costs. Costs refer to the value of all of the resources used in the evaluation, including the time of participants, subjects, and volunteer workers; and the services contributed to the evaluation by any other agencies, whether or not they appear in the evaluation budget. That is, costs refer to the total value, social and monetary, of all the human and physical resources used to carry out the evaluation. Benefits denote the value of all the results derived from the evaluation: these include, but are not limited to, the value of correctly diagnosing and treating students' educational problems and needs, publicly identifying effective and ineffective educational goods and services, determining accurately whether institutions and programs are qualified to perform specified educational functions, discovering how the monetary and non-monetary costs of a program might be reduced without decreasing its services, and fostering understanding of activities and how they are perceived in a given setting and from a variety of perspectives.

Often evaluators have under consideration several alternative designs they could choose for conducting an evaluation. If none is judged cost effective and no additional designs are identified, then the evaluation should not be undertaken. If only one is judged cost effective, then it obviously should be selected. But if more than one are judged cost effective, then the design with the best combination of costs and benefits should be chosen. When a more costly evaluation is expected to provide the most useful information, the evaluator and client must decide whether the extra information is worth the extra expense. If the benefits are judged equal for alternative designs, the choice can be made on the basis of cost alone.

**Guidelines**   A. Investigate thoroughly initial costs of materials and services to be used (e.g., answer sheets, copy paper, interviewer time, and films); and project future cost trends.

B. Make an inventory of evaluation costs, including dollar amounts (from Guideline A), time, and other resources of participants, and human disaffection.

C. Make an inventory of benefits—those agreed upon with the client, as well as beneficial side effects for other audiences (e.g., increased interest of parents in a program or improvement of students' attitudes toward evaluation).

D. Before deciding to do an evaluation, weigh anticipated costs against projected benefits to the client and other relevant audiences.

E. Conduct evaluations as economically as possible.

**Pitfalls**   A. Conducting an evaluation because it is required when it obviously cannot yield useful results

B. Selecting an evaluation design that is familiar without searching for alternatives that are more cost effective

C. Commencing an evaluation without a commitment of sufficient resources to carry it through

D. Assuming that an initial heavy outlay of resources obviates the need to ensure that the evaluation will be cost effective

**Caveats**   A. Remember that concern for cost effectiveness should not deter evaluators from trying new methods or doing evaluations that are important but difficult to do. And it must not turn evaluations into predictable, routine, pedestrian inquiries.

B. Recognize that cost effectiveness analysis is not easily adaptable to education, since educational outcomes are numerous, intangible, and differentially valued by different groups, and since often they are not easily translated into numbers.

**Illustrative Case**   A superintendent contracted for an evaluation of a new elementary school mathematics program. The purpose of the evaluation was to assess the program as a whole. While a part of the evaluation was the assessment of the computational skills of the district's third-grade and fourth-grade students, the performance of individual students was not at issue. In fact, only district-level results were to be reported.

A committee of teachers selected a set of 300 computational problems which were judged to be appropriate for assessing the degree to which 30 computational objectives of the mathematics program were being met.

The evaluators combined the 300 problems into a test which required three sessions of two and one-half hours each to administer. This test was given to all third-grade and fourth-grade students in the district.

**Analysis of the Case**    While accomplishing the goal of assessing the degree to which the 30 computational objectives had been achieved, the evaluation required the investment of more student and teacher time than was necessary. This was especially true, since the scores of individual students were not reported.

Rather than constructing a single test of 300 problems, the evaluators might have randomly divided the problems into ten subsets of 30 problems each. The ten subsets could have been randomly assigned and administered to students in a random sample of classrooms, so that each participating student responded to a single subset of 30 items. Substantial savings of pupil and teacher time could have been achieved with little loss in the accuracy of the assessment.

# C
# PROPRIETY STANDARDS

## SUMMARY OF THE STANDARDS

### C Propriety Standards

The Propriety Standards are intended to ensure that an evaluation will be conducted legally, ethically, and with due regard for the welfare of those involved in the evaluation, as well as those affected by its results. These standards are:

### C1 Formal Obligation

Obligations of the formal parties to an evaluation (what is to be done, how, by whom, when) should be agreed to in writing, so that these parties are obligated to adhere to all conditions of the agreement or formally to renegotiate it.

### C2 Conflict of Interest

Conflict of interest, frequently unavoidable, should be dealt with openly and honestly, so that it does not compromise the evaluation processes and results.

### C3 Full and Frank Disclosure

Oral and written evaluation reports should be open, direct, and honest in their disclosure of pertinent findings, including the limitations of the evaluation.

### C4  Public's Right to Know

The formal parties to an evaluation should respect and assure the public's right to know, within the limits of other related principles and statutes, such as those dealing with public safety and the right to privacy.

### C5  Rights of Human Subjects

Evaluations should be designed and conducted, so that the rights and welfare of the human subjects are respected and protected.

### C6  Human Interactions

Evaluators should respect human dignity and worth in their interactions with other persons associated with an evaluation.

### C7  Balanced Reporting

The evaluation should be complete and fair in its presentation of strengths and weaknesses of the object under investigation, so that strengths can be built upon and problem areas addressed.

### C8  Fiscal Responsibility

The evaluator's allocation and expenditure of resources should reflect sound accountability procedures and otherwise be prudent and ethically responsible.

# C1 FORMAL OBLIGATION

**Standard**  Obligations of the formal parties to an evaluation (what is to be done, how, by whom, when) should be agreed to in writing, so that these parties are obligated to adhere to all conditions of the agreement or formally to renegotiate it.

**Overview**  A written agreement is a mutual understanding of specified expectations and responsibilities of both client and evaluator. Having entered into such an agreement, both parties have a legal and ethical obligation to carry it out in a forthright manner or to renegotiate it. Neither party is obligated to honor decisions made unilaterally by the other.

Guidelines of federal, state, and local agencies for external evaluations often require that evaluator and client enter into formal contract. But even when a formal contract is not mandated—commonly the case with internal evaluations—the parties to the evaluation should develop at least a brief memorandum of agreement spelling out what is to be done, by whom, how, and when.

School districts may deal systematically with evaluation contract issues by having their boards adopt policies pertaining to such matters as: responsibilities of district personnel for conducting and participating in evaluations; approval of evaluation plans; protection of human subjects; data collection, storage and retrieval; editing and disseminating reports; use of external evaluators; and financing the evaluation effort.

Both client and evaluator usually begin their relationship in an atmosphere of mutual respect and confidence. This is the best atmosphere in which to negotiate a contract (or to establish general policies) to guide the behavior of both. The process of developing a written agreement provides evaluator and client the opportunity to review and summarize the total evaluation plan and to clarify their respective rights and responsibilities in the enterprise. A formal agreement can reduce and help resolve many of the day-to-day misunderstandings between evaluator and client, and, if serious misunderstandings occur, it can help resolve them. As an appendix to the final evaluation report, the evaluation contract or memorandum of agreement can promote understanding of the agreements that guided the evaluation.

**Guidelines**    A. Include in the agreement (allowing for appropriate adjustments in emergent designs):

1. objectives of the evaluation;

2. questions to be investigated;

3. data collection procedures, including data and data sources, sample size and selection, instruments and other data-gathering techniques, and any site-visiting plan;

4. data analysis procedures, including descriptive and comparative, statistical and nonstatistical;

5. reporting plan, including a consideration of report format and delivery (number and types of reports, length, audiences, and methods of presentation), anonymity of subjects/respondents, prerelease review of reports, rebuttal by those being evaluated, and editorial and final release authority over completed reports;

6. methods for controlling and assessing bias in data collection, analysis, and reporting;

7. services, personnel, information, and materials provided by clients, including access to data;

8. timeline for work of both clients and evaluators;

9. contract amendment and termination procedures; and

10. budget for the work, including amounts to be paid upon completion of certain tasks or on specified dates.

B. Establish, within reasonable limits, what would constitute a breach of the agreement by either party and what consequent actions may be taken.

C. Ensure that the agreement conforms to federal and state statutes and local regulations applying to such contractual arrangements.

D. Have an outside party—an attorney, if appropriate—review the agreement for clarity and soundness.

E. Negotiate amendments as the work proceeds if changing circumstances make alterations in work scope, cost, or timetable necessary or desirable.

F. Collaborate with educational administrators in drafting policies for board approval covering the conduct of the evaluation.

**Pitfalls**  A. Allowing the original proposal to constitute the full written agreement

B. Failing to consult with those who will be directly affected by the contract but who are not signatories—school principals and teachers, for example—before the agreement is signed (see A1, Audience Identification, A2, Evaluator Credibility, and B2, Political Viability)

C. Expecting performance by parties not under the control of the signatories without consulting these parties

D. Acting unilaterally in any matter where it has been agreed that evaluator/client collaboration would be required for decisions

E. Changing the design, scope, or cost of the study without officially amending the agreement

**Caveats**  A. Do not adhere so rigidly to the contract that changes dictated by common sense are not made or are unduly delayed.

B. Do not develop contracts that are so detailed that they stifle the creativity of the evaluation team or require an undue amount of time and resources in their development.

**Illustrative Case**  A state education association, concerned about the ways in which school districts were holding teachers accountable for professional performance, decided to undertake a thorough appraisal of those procedures. Accordingly, an evaluation organization was commissioned for the task.

The state education association and the evaluators assumed that a formal agreement would be necessary before the study commenced. However, what should be included in the agreement was never fully addressed. Early discussions between the evaluators and the association authorities centered on procedures to be pursued in conducting the study, rather than on specific agreements about who would do what, for what reasons, and at what times. When the formal agreement was completed, both parties felt confident that the important issues had been covered.

Following a comprehensive investigation of accountability procedures used by school districts, the evaluators presented the report, as agreed, to education association authorities. The findings indicated that the school districts had employed inadequate and unreliable teacher-appraisal instruments, and that association officials had contributed to the general failure of the accountability strategies by encouraging teachers not to cooperate with school districts' initiatives to hold teachers professionally accountable.

As agreed contractually, the report was disseminated to specified audiences by the education association authorities according to a prearranged time schedule. The evaluators soon discovered that those sections which were critical of the teachers' association had been removed from the report. Moreover, the evaluators were at a serious disadvantage in seeking redress because the matter of final editorial authority had not been included in the formal agreement. At this point, the evaluators' options were limited to submitting to the action of the association or publicly condemning the behavior of the association officials.

**Analysis of the Case**   During preliminary discussions with the state education association authorities, the evaluators should have taken careful note of points for inclusion in the formal agreement, including possible difficulties arising from the controversial nature of the subject. Mutual agreement should have been reached, so that all crucial issues had been fully and fairly settled in the contract. When near completion, the contract should have been scrutinized by both parties and consideration given to the possibility of review by legal experts.

Under such an agreement, if the education association authorities had tried to persuade the evaluators to modify the report before it was disseminated, they could have refused to do so. No doubt, they would have concluded that the integrity of the report would be damaged by the requested modifications. The evaluators' final editorial authority, by this contract, would have assured the right to contest the issues.

# C2 CONFLICT OF INTEREST

**Standard**   Conflict of interest, frequently unavoidable, should be dealt with openly and honestly, so that it does not compromise the evaluation processes and results.

**Overview**   Conflict of interest exists in an evaluation when the evaluators' private interests might be affected by their evaluative actions. For example:

1. The evaluators might be able to advance their particular philosophical, theoretical, or political point of view by reporting particular findings.

2. They might benefit or lose financially, long-term or short-term, depending on what evaluation results they report, especially if the evaluators are connected financially to the object of the evaluation or to one of its competitors.

3. The evaluators' jobs and/or ability to get future evaluation contracts might be influenced by their reporting of either positive or negative findings.

4. The evaluators' personal or political ties to their client might be strengthened or weakened by reporting results that reflect positively or negatively on the client.

5. The evaluators' agency might stand to gain or lose, especially if they trained the personnel or developed the materials involved in the object of the evaluation.

The breadth of the above examples indicates that many evaluations contain the potential for conflict of interest; thus, the problem is frequently not a matter of how to avoid conflict of interest but of how to deal with it. It is a prevalent concern in internal evaluations where close friendships and personal working relations are commonplace and may influence the outcomes of the evaluations. It is also a frequent problem in external evaluations, since clients have much freedom to choose external evaluators and external evaluators must win evaluation contracts in order to stay in business. Conflicts of interest can bias evaluations by corrupting their processes, findings, and interpretations.

**Guidelines**  A. In initial discussions with clients, identify and clearly describe possible sources of conflict of interest.

B. Seek advice from persons who have different perspectives on the evaluation in order to stay open to evaluation alternatives and philosophies and thus plan and conduct a less-biased evaluation.

C. Release evaluation procedures, data, and reports publicly, so they can be judged by other independent evaluators.

D. Agree in writing on procedures to protect against problems associated with conflict of interest in methodology or reporting (see C1, Formal Obligation).

E. Whenever possible, obtain the evaluation contract from the funding agency directly, rather than through the funded project.

F. Assess what advantages (monetary, social, moral, political) various parties may gain or lose as a result of the evaluation and be prepared to resist pressures they might exert.

G. Make internal evaluators directly responsible to agency heads, thus limiting the influence which other agency staff might have on the evaluators.

**Pitfalls**  A. Believing that calling the attention of officials of the client agency to a real or potential conflict of interest within the agency or its constituency will be sufficient to correct the problem (public disclosure or corrective action cannot always be expected, since it may reflect adversely on the officials or the agency)

B. Assuming that merely following a set of well-established "objective" procedures will eliminate all conflicts of interest

C. Assuming that independent, nationally known experts are unbiased and free from conflict of interest problems

**Caveat**  A. Take care not to exclude persons who are uniquely qualified to be involved in the evaluation solely because of the fear of conflict of interest allegations.

**Illustrative Case**  A school district curriculum director had worked with the system's reading specialists and teachers to develop a curriculum guide and materials for a three-stage individualized reading program in grades 1–4.

The director commissioned outside evaluators to evaluate the first stage, with the idea that if their work was satisfactory they would be engaged for the second and third stage evaluations— with considerably larger contracts. The evaluators soon realized that the curriculum director had been the major architect of the new curriculum guide and accompanying materials, that he believed strongly in their value, and that he would play a key role in awarding contracts for evaluations of the second and third stages of the program.

Rather than involving the reading specialists and school staffs directly in developing criteria for evaluating the guide and materials, the evaluators created a design that emphasized the strongest aspects of the guide and minimized its weaknesses. In addition, the evaluators added a person to their team who had previously served as a consultant to the curriculum director in the development of the guide and materials.

The evaluation report was highly favorable. However, when it was released, a substantial number of teachers complained to the superintendent of schools that major controversial elements of the curriculum guide as well as deficiencies in the materials had been glossed over during the evaluation, that the objectives of the teachers themselves had not been properly considered, and that one of the evaluators had been influential in writing the curriculum guide.

The superintendent concluded that the evaluators had been too eager to win future contracts, had compromised their objectivity, and had destroyed their credibility. He directed that they not be engaged further.

**Analysis of the Case**    At the beginning the evaluators should have assessed and dealt openly with their own potential conflict of interest, that of their client, and those of other involved parties. If they were not successful in instituting procedures that would keep the evaluation reasonably free from being influenced to serve vested interests, they should have declined to proceed with the evaluation. Certainly they should not have designed and staffed the evaluation so that a positive report was virtually assured.

They might have involved the reading specialists, the curriculum director, and the teachers in developing criteria for assessing the curriculum guide and accompanying materials. They then could have developed a design by which to describe and assess the guide and materials; and they could have collected and reported judgments of the materials from a wide spectrum of participants in the reading program.

# C3 FULL AND FRANK DISCLOSURE

**Standard**    Oral and written evaluation reports should be open, direct, and honest in their disclosure of pertinent findings, including the limitations of the evaluation.

**Overview**    Full and frank disclosure means telling what one thinks and believes, as candidly as possible, based on one's best informed judgment. It requires that all acts, public pronouncements, and written reports of the evaluation adhere strictly to a code of directness, openness, and completeness.

Full and frank disclosure in reporting is essential if the evaluation is to be defensible. Its absence will severely threaten the evaluation's credibility. Audiences for the evaluation are entitled to reports that present clearly and frankly the evaluator's judgments and recommendations, and the information that was used to formulate them. Such reporting at the developmental stages may contribute substantially to bringing about needed program changes.

**Guidelines**    A. Report completely, orally and in writing, with full disclosure of pertinent findings and without omissions or other alterations based solely on the evaluator's opinions.

B. Show clearly the basis for the perceived relationship between the objectives of the evaluation, the data collected, and the findings (see D10, Justified Conclusions).

C. Present relevant points of view of both supporters and critics of the program being evaluated (see A3, Information Scope and Selection).

D. Report key factors which might significantly detract from or add to the evaluation's validity, whether discovered before or during the evaluation, and discuss frankly their implications for the findings and recommendations (see D2, Context Analysis).

E. Report judgments and recommendations that represent broad, balanced, and informed perspectives.

**Pitfall**  A. Issuing reports which have been altered to reflect the self-interest of the evaluator, the client, or the program staff

**Caveats**  A. Do not confuse full and frank disclosure with premature disclosure of information in a condition that may lead to misinterpretation and misunderstanding.

B. Do not make so much of the limitations that the report will fail to gain the credibility it deserves.

C. Do not concentrate so heavily on being candid that the rights of persons involved in the evaluation are violated (see C1, Formal Obligation and C5, Rights of Human Subjects).

D. Do not design evaluations and construct and release reports without considering pertinent social and political factors (see D2, Context Analysis).

**Illustrative Case**  A staff evaluator was asked to develop an evaluation report covering the first year's operation of the USOE-funded early childhood education project in a native American community. While examining the data the evaluator discovered that parental involvement, crucial to carrying out certain features of the program in the home setting, had been seriously compromised because a small minority of parents opposed some of the program's basic assumptions and tenets. Consequently, not all of the program's first-year objectives had been met, and it was dubious whether the second year's activities could be mounted as originally planned.

The evaluator, concerned that the funding might not be renewed if the dissension were reported, omitted discussion of its negative effects. The evaluator rationalized his behavior to himself by arguing that, after all, the project would be evaluated in a full, summative report at the end of the second year; that there was no point in "throwing out the baby with the bath"; that project personnel were well-intentioned and deserved the opportunity to show what they could do; and that premature close-down of the project would unnecessarily disrupt the incomes and lives of the staff.

Full and frank presentation of the evaluation data, in all aspects, was thus compromised. The audiences, including project staff, were lulled into believing that all was well. Corrective actions could not be taken, and needed improvements were delayed. Further, the concerns and issues of the dissident parents were not addressed, so that it became likely that the disruptions would be repeated again during the second year. All in all, the probability was greatly increased that the project would fail, that possibly useful practices would be discarded, that potential adoptions in other settings would be aborted, and that the federal investment would be wasted.

**Analysis of the Case**   The evaluator should have reported all the findings openly and honestly. He should have realized that the judgment he made to suppress certain information was not his to make; indeed, that it bordered on the unethical even though his motives may have been good. He might have offered to work with both the project staff and the dissident parents in characterizing their differences more sharply and to collect information pertinent to those differences that would facilitate appropriate adjustments and refinements.

# C4 PUBLIC'S RIGHT TO KNOW

**Standard**     The formal parties to an evaluation should respect and assure the public's right to know, within the limits of other related principles and statutes, such as those dealing with public safety and the right to privacy.

**Overview**     A "right-to-know" audience is one that is entitled ethically and legally to be informed about the intents, operations, and outcomes of an evaluation. The principle that defines a right-to-know audience is that those persons who will be affected by the evaluation should be informed about how and why it was done and about its results, except where the disclosure of such information would endanger public safety or abridge individual freedoms.

If persons or groups who will be affected by the evaluation cannot get information about it, they cannot detect flaws in its procedures or data, nor can they make constructive use of its findings. As a consequence, these persons may unwittingly become the victims of unwarranted conclusions and actions, or may perform their functions less well than they might have had they been informed of the evaluation findings. Evaluations should be expected to withstand the critical examination of those whose lives they may affect and to provide them with useful information.

The evaluator's ability to identify and properly serve right-to-know audiences greatly influences the fairness and utility of the evaluation. In turn, the evaluator's ability to release information is often partially controlled by the client. Therefore, both the evaluator and client bear responsibility for meeting this standard.

**Guidelines**     A. Advocate the public's right to know. Encourage clients to provide constituents—pupils, parents, teachers, administrators, other employees, board members, and citizens—information that is appropriate and timely, and that helps them to be enlightened contributors, consumers, critics, and observers.

B. Become knowledgeable about the statutes bearing on the public's right to know, and how these statutes relate to (and are tempered by) other statutes on privacy rights, civil and human rights, health, safety, etc.

C. Reach a formal agreement with the client during the planning stages of the evaluation covering the client's and evaluator's roles in assuring compliance with right-to-know requirements, including: identification of audiences for interim and final reports; authority to edit reports; documentation of intents, procedures and outcomes; and when, how, and to whom information about the evaluation will be released (see C1, Formal Obligation).

**Pitfalls**  A. Determining right-to-know audiences on the basis of convenience or economy, rather than ethical and legal considerations

B. Failing to be involved in the control and release of information about, or resulting from, the evaluation

C. Agreeing to allow the client to select and release parts of the evaluation report without consulting the evaluator (see C1, Formal Obligation)

D. Giving the client unilateral authority to edit, censor, or in any other way change the evaluation report before its release (see C1, Formal Obligation)

E. Releasing information or endorsing the client's release of information to selected members of the right-to-know audience, while withholding the information from other members of this audience

F. Releasing partial information that has been selected to serve the client's personal needs, beliefs, or professional biases

**Caveats**  A. Do not violate any individual's right to privacy (see C5, Rights of Human Subjects).

B. Be considerate of the client's rights, responsibilities, and needs (see C6, Human Interactions).

**Illustrative Case**  For almost two years, the residents of a school district had been clamoring against the injustices of the district's desegregation strategies. The most prominent minority group insisted that integration plans were a farce, while the majority group was equally vehement that there was a reverse discrimination favoring the minority children. The board of education decided to have the situation evaluated so that problems might be placed openly in their proper perspective. Moreover, it was hoped that as a result of an evaluation, decisions could be made which would alleviate the tense situation.

The evaluators selected were not knowledgeable about the laws governing the public's right to know. They had never been challenged over information disclosure and did not consider this aspect of an evaluation to be important.

In the formal agreement with the school board, the evaluators did not concern themselves with the matter of information dissemination to the public. Interested parties, the agreement stated, would be "informed of outcomes of the evaluation in due course and at the discretion of the Board." Although the evaluators soon became aware that negative feelings were running high between the minority and majority groups in relation to desegregation issues, they concentrated on the school situation and almost totally ignored parents and the public at all stages of the evaluation.

A report was eventually submitted to the board. After some changes had been made in deference to the board's requests (for example, elimination of the mention of questionable decisions about busing), the evaluators presented their findings at a public meeting. A large crowd attended, demanding to know why they had not been consulted about the planning of the evaluation, why they had not been involved, why intermediate reports had not been released, and why the final report failed to address questions about the propriety of board decisions on busing. The evaluators and board were accused of violating laws covering public disclosure of information and their credibility and integrity were questioned.

**Analysis of the Case**    The evaluators, whether or not they sensed the intensity of public interest over the desegregation issue, should have made sure that the formal agreement with the school board complied with federal and state laws relating to disclosure of public information. With the board's concurrence, the evaluators might have formed an advisory group—consisting of representatives of the school and community—and consulted them about what questions should be addressed in the evaluation.

During the course of the evaluation, intermediate reports might have been issued relating to completed aspects of the evaluation which could be pursued as entities—one dealing with a history of busing and the other with curricular offerings at the various schools within the district. Representatives of both the minority and majority groups could have been invited to respond to these reports as well as to other important findings during the course of the evaluation.

The final report should have been presented to the open, public meeting without being altered, even though many of the recommendations might have been unpalatable to either group, and to the board. If the public had been kept openly, honestly, and objectively informed at all stages of the evaluation, the report likely would have been accepted by more people and its credibility would not have been so susceptible to attack.

# C5 RIGHTS OF HUMAN SUBJECTS

**Standard**  Evaluations should be designed and conducted so that the rights and welfare of the human subjects are respected and protected.

**Overview**  Rights of human subjects in an evaluation include those rights which apply specifically to their being part of the evaluation and those generic rights which apply to many other situations. Some such rights are based in law, and some in accepted ethical practice, common sense, and courtesy. Legal provisions bearing on rights of human subjects include those dealing with consent (of subject, parents, or guardians) for participation, privilege of withdrawal, privacy of certain thoughts and information, confidentiality of some information, and health and safety protections. Ethical and common sense considerations include the right to determine one's physical and emotional preparedness for treatment, to place limits on time spans of involvement, and generally to avoid physically harmful or uncomfortable experiences.

Evaluators, for both moral and pragmatic reasons, should be knowledgeable about and adhere to both the legal and other human rights requirements of their evaluations. Those who are not informed about the rights of human subjects may unwittingly ignore or abuse them and harm the participants in the evaluation. If evaluators violate legal and ethical rights, knowingly or not, they will be subject to legal prosecution and/or professional sanctions. Regardless of whether the violations are conscious or the violators are punished, the injured participants may become opponents of educational evaluation generally. In addition, some audiences may discount conclusions and recommendations if they learn that these were derived from information obtained illegally or unethically.

**Guidelines**  A. Be aware that the rights of human beings are either explicit or implied in many moral, ethical, and legal codes (e.g., amendments to the Constitution).

B. Be knowledgeable about due process and civil rights laws.

C. Before initiating an evaluation, determine which ethical and legal principles apply to it.

D. Do not deprive students of instructional methods that are normally available to them and that are known to be beneficial. For instance, students should not be assigned (randomly or otherwise) to a control group in which instruction previously available from public resources (such as the services of certified teachers or use of library materials) is purposely withheld to assess the effect of such deprivation.

E. Develop formal written agreements that explain the procedures that will be followed by the client and the evaluator to ensure that the rights of human subjects will be protected.

F. Immediately inform individuals and/or parents or guardians when it is intended that they are to become subjects.

G. Inform subjects and/or parents or guardians of their rights in the evaluation (e.g., that they can withdraw from the evaluation at any time without penalty or prejudice).

H. When permission of parents or guardians is needed in an evaluation (e.g., to test children) the evaluator should thoroughly inform the parents of the implications of the evaluation and should obtain a signed form from them giving permission to test the children. It is not enough to assume permission simply because parents or guardians do not specifically object to their children being tested.

I. Obtain appropriate written permission from relevant authorities (e.g., the subjects themselves, their parents or guardians, or relevant administrative authorities) for access to individual records.

J. When anonymity is guaranteed to those individuals who supply information for use in the evaluation, set up a procedure to guarantee that this anonymity will be protected (e.g., mark individual data records with identifying numbers rather than names, appoint an independent escrow agent to keep the only list that links the numbers to the names, and arrange for the destruction of the list when it is no longer required).

K. In reporting the evaluation findings, sufficiently disguise the identities of individuals so that they cannot be identified from contextual clues.

L. Guard against the possibility that other parties will use the collected data for purposes different from those agreed to by the persons who provided the data.

**Pitfalls**  A. Promising confidentiality when it cannot be guaranteed

B. Guaranteeing that information will be used only to serve the stated purposes, when the courts may legally order that the information be released to serve other purposes

C. Failing to communicate clearly how the information which persons are willing to provide will be used and the extent to which it can be kept confidential

D. Jeopardizing the self-esteem and reputations of participants by publishing a report that questions their professional ability or their personal ethics without giving them an opportunity to present their perspective

**Caveats**  A. Do not choose methods that theoretically are the best for obtaining unequivocal information if they have a significant potential for violating the rights of human subjects.

B. Beyond obtaining informed consents, weigh human costs against benefits, and consider not doing the evaluation if the benefits do not justify the costs.

C. Accord program administrators the right to remain silent on personal matters, but require them to give access to information about program effectiveness even if they consider it personally threatening.

D. Respect the right of those who carry out the program, such as teachers or tutors, legitimately to avoid supplying information about their effectiveness if they were not involved in planning the program and/or if they had no control over how it was implemented.

E. Do not allow one's inability to guarantee that no person's rights will be violated to prevent the implementation of needed evaluations. While it may not be possible to eliminate all violations of human rights, reasonable precautions should be put into effect.

**Illustrative Case**  A board of education decided to examine which of three different approaches to education ("traditional," "fundamental," and "experimental") worked best with which kinds of students. The district hired an evaluator who recommended that a stratified random sampling plan be used to assign students to schools representing the different approaches. Stratification variables included measures of students' personality, achievement, and socioeconomic characteristics. Included in the data collected from students was such sensitive information as how much money their parents earned per year.

Although there was a clear directive in the evaluation agreement to obtain prior approval from the district superintendent or her designated representative before any measures were administered to students, the evaluator decided to bypass this restriction in some instances in order to complete data collection in time to meet other contractual agreements. The evaluator carried out parts of the testing program under the guise of field testing "draft" instruments.

Shortly after the data were collected, a principal at one school requested a particular student's scores on one of the experimental personality measures used for the evaluation, so that he could better understand why the student was frequently in trouble. The evaluator was happy to comply with this request, as doing so might improve worsening relations between the evaluator and the district staff.

The evaluator decided to discuss that student's data in the final report to illustrate specific findings. In doing so, she provided enough information to reveal the student's identity to anyone casually acquainted with the student. The parents of the student sued the school district for rights violations.

**Analysis of the Case**  All data collection instruments should have been considered and approved prior to their use. Time to carry out this process should have been anticipated by the evaluator in setting up the schedule of activities. If delays developed, the evaluator could have impressed upon the superintendent the impact of ignoring or circumventing those rights to expedite completion of the evaluation.

The principal's request for information about a particular student should have been denied because of restrictions regarding the confidentiality of such data. The restrictions also should have guided the evaluator's judgments regarding how to discuss particular cases, teachers, and schools in the final evaluation report.

# C6 HUMAN INTERACTIONS

**Standard**     Evaluators should respect human dignity and worth in their interactions with other persons associated with an evaluation.

**Overview**     Human interaction in the context of this standard pertains to evaluators' interpersonal transactions which affect the feelings and self-respect of those who participate in an evaluation. Most evaluations have the potential for reflecting either positively or negatively on individuals or groups and their work. The point of this standard is that evaluators must guard against the potentially harmful effects of their human interactions.

Evaluators who do not understand and respect the feelings of participants in an evaluation may needlessly sadden or harm these persons, or provoke in them hostility towards the evaluation. Such offense to people violates the moral imperative that human beings' essential dignity must be respected, and it inhibits human creativity. In addition, it is impractical, because participants who have been offended may be moved to do things that seriously jeopardize the evaluation. Evaluators should make a balanced effort to show respect for participants in an evaluation and should develop sound evaluative conclusions and recommendations.

**Guidelines**     A. Make every effort to understand the cultural and social values of the participants, particularly if their values are pluralistic or different from the evaluators' values (see A4, Valuational Interpretation).

B. Take time to learn from the participants their particular concerns about the evaluation (see A1, Audience Identification, A3, Information Scope and Selection, and B2, Political Viability).

C. Maintain good communication about the evaluation with participants through established channels.

D. Become familiar with the organization where the evaluation is to be done, and plan the evaluation activities for minimum disruption of the organization's staff procedures, routines, and work schedules (see D2, Context Analysis).

**Pitfalls**     A. Behaving attentively and respectfully toward those in positions of authority while largely ignoring their subordinates

B. Assigning greater or lesser importance to some persons because of their age, sex, or race

C. Violating legal requirements or protocol in contacting and addressing participants

D. Reporting findings as personal evaluations of, or attacks on, people involved in the program being evaluated

E. Discussing one's attitudes about the personal attributes—such as intelligence, physical attractiveness, taste, and social skills—of persons whose work is being evaluated

**Caveats**     A. Consider not collecting information which might embarrass participants, if this information is not essential, if it might be collected in an equally useful form that would protect the identity of the participants, and if not collecting it might, in the long run, be more beneficial to the evaluation or the program being evaluated.

B. Do not go to such lengths to avoid embarrassing people or hurting their feelings that the validity and utility of the evaluation are sacrificed and the findings are not reported honestly, or that incompetence or unethical behavior by program participants is covered up.

**Illustrative Case**     A university's curriculum department undertook an evaluation to determine the impact of a history course on the achievement of poverty-level secondary school students. By arrangement with the curriculum department and its team of evaluators, a local school district agreed to participate in the evaluation.

The evaluators developed an operational definition of a poverty-level student, identified all the students in the eleventh grade in the participating district who met this definition, then randomly assigned half of these students to be taught by the history course.

All the poverty-level students who had been identified were convened at the beginning and at the end of the evaluation for testing. On each occasion, they were told that they would be tested to help the evaluators determine the effectiveness of the school district's programs for serving the needs of disadvantaged students.

In addition to the testing, the evaluation design included extensive classroom observation and pupil interviews. To ensure that the teachers would not make unusual preparations for the observations, the evaluators visited classrooms unannounced and conducted their observations without any advance agreements with either the teachers or their school principals. Similarly, the evaluators went unannounced to the homes of students to interview them about their school experiences.

When the final report was published, criticisms of the evaluators' insensitivities towards participants began to arrive at the school district's central office. The critics charged, for example, that the evaluators had:

1. disconcerted teachers by extensive classroom observation;

2. made thinly veiled criticisms to some teachers about their implementation of the history course; and

3. caused acute embarrassment to poverty-level pupils by separating them from other pupils, publicly labeling them as disadvantaged, and intruding on their homes unannounced.

In the light of these persistent criticisms, the school administration and the board tended to place less confidence than they might have in the evaluators and thus in the report. Later, they discounted the report altogether when they learned that the teachers and students who allegedly had been demeaned had not cooperated with the evaluators. As a consequence of these problems, the relationship between the university and the school district was weakened.

**Analysis of the Case**    The evaluators should have realized that their evaluation would have to be handled carefully—particularly with respect to poverty-level students. They might have selected students randomly from the total student population and assured that no students were labeled or identified publicly with respect to income level or other sensitive characteristics. The test results then could have been analyzed and reported so as to assess the program's comparative effects on poverty-level and nonpoverty-level students without embarrassing any student. In any case, the students' names and test scores should not have been revealed. The interviews with students probably should have been conducted privately in the students' schools; if there was a compelling reason to use their homes, these interviews should have been arranged carefully with the full knowledge and consent of the students, parents, and school officials.

Teachers and school principals should have been involved in the planning of various aspects of the evaluation, especially concerning the classroom observations. Conferences involving teachers, principals, and the evaluators could have been held periodically to report progress and to deal with problems, fears, threats, and insecurities. If some teachers had expressed embarrassment at overambitious observing and probing by the evaluators, an alternative strategy could have been agreed upon.

Given these procedures, strong recommendations for use of the history course for poverty-level students might have gained general support among teachers when the report was disseminated, and beneficial change could have occurred.

# C7 BALANCED REPORTING

**Standard**   The evaluation should be complete and fair in its presentation of strengths and weaknesses of the object under investigation, so that strengths can be built upon and problem areas addressed.

**Overview**   Balancing an evaluation does not mean generating equal numbers of strengths and weaknesses. It means being complete and fair in assessing and reporting both negative and positive aspects of the object being evaluated.

Even if the primary purpose of an evaluation is to determine the weaknesses of an object, it is essential to identify strengths as well. One reason for this is that strengths can sometimes be used to correct weaknesses. Another is that actions taken to correct weaknesses may inadvertently diminish some unidentified strengths.

**Guidelines**   A. Report findings which indicate either strengths or weaknesses, whether intended or unintended, and identify where each is substantiated.

B. List key characteristics of the object and, using one or more perspectives, classify each as a strength, weakness, or neutral feature (see C1, Formal Obligation).

C. Within limits of time and resources, before submitting the final report, solicit critical comments from knowledgeable parties representing diverse perspectives about the balance of strengths and weaknesses.

D. When some kinds of relevant data are inaccessible because of time or cost constraints, report these omissions, estimating their effect on the overall judgment of the object if they were either strongly positive or negative.

**Pitfalls**　A. Manipulating the balance of strengths and weaknesses to please partisan interest groups or allowing these groups to delete from the report weaknesses which might prove embarrassing

B. Manipulating the balance of strengths and weaknesses to further or protect the evaluator's personal interests or biases

C. Reporting a value judgment as either a strength or weakness without considering alternative perspectives which might change that conclusion

**Caveat**　A. Do not report highly tentative findings for the purpose of achieving balance; if the body of defensible findings reveals an imbalance of strengths and weaknesses, that should be reflected in the report.

**Illustrative Case**　An external evaluation group was hired to evaluate a two-week workshop which trained teachers to teach in teams. The trainers' materials and the teachers' materials developed for the workshop were the objects of the evaluation. The evaluation group was asked to find the weaknesses in the materials and to suggest improvements. Following the workshop, the evaluators interviewed the trainers and the teachers to discover deficiencies in the materials and collect suggestions for changes.

The report listed the weaknesses and recommended changes to correct them. Later, when the developers of the materials tried to use the report to guide revisions, they discovered that making the recommended changes would destroy characteristics they considered to be primary strengths of the materials. However, the report offered no data on whether the trainers and teachers shared that view or how these characteristics related to the identified weaknesses. Lacking that balance, the report could not be used as a blueprint for revising the materials.

**Analysis of the Case**　The evaluators could have asked the trainers and the teachers to identify both strengths and weaknesses in the materials, and to rate sections of the materials on their effectiveness or usability. Furthermore, the evaluators could have gathered empirical data on how the materials were, in fact, used during the workshop and on whether teachers learned what the materials were designed to teach them.

The final report could have analyzed the relative strengths and weaknesses reported by those who used the materials, substantiated by data on the actual effects of the materials in producing skillful teachers with favorable attitudes toward team teaching. The materials then could have been revised accordingly.

# C8 FISCAL RESPONSIBILITY

**Standard** The evaluator's allocation and expenditure of resources should reflect sound accountability procedures and otherwise be prudent and ethically responsible.

**Overview** Evaluators are fiscally accountable when funds are used for the purposes and procedures stated in the evaluation agreement, expenditures are in compliance with pertinent state and federal statutes and associated rules and regulations, and financial transactions are verified by standard accounting and auditing procedures.

There is always the possibility that evaluators will misuse the funds for which they are responsible; in addition, certain groups or individuals, attempting to discredit an evaluation, find funding a tempting area to exploit. Therefore, it is important that evaluators exercise extreme care in their use and accounting of funds.

**Guidelines** A. Maintain accurate records of sources of funding and expenditures in a clear and understandable format.

b. Maintain adequate personnel records with respect to job allocations and time spent on the job.

C. Be efficient without compromising the quality of the evaluation.

D. Specify major costs for the evaluation in agreements with the clients, including personnel, consultants, travel, supplies, postage, telephone, data processing, conferences and meetings, public information, printing, meta evaluation, and overhead (see C1, Formal Obligation).

E. Use contract bidding or comparison shopping for the purchase of resources and services.

F. Include an expenditure summary as part of the public report to enhance public confidence in the evaluation. If private evaluators prefer not to do this, they should, at a minimum, have such data available upon request.

**Pitfalls**  A. Commencing a study without a carefully planned budget

B. Changing the evaluation activity plan without making necessary budgetary adjustments

C. Being unaware of laws applicable to the expenditure of funds

D. Becoming encumbered with unethical ties of any nature related to the appropriation or use of funds

**Caveats**  A. Ensure that the budget is sufficiently flexible or renegotiable that reallocations can be made in the interests of successfully completing the evaluation or directly benefiting the program being evaluated.

B. Discuss openly and frankly with clients unexpected occurrences which threaten the financial viability of the evaluation. For example, salaries of project personnel may increase steeply because of an unexpected award in collective bargaining. Make an effort to achieve an equitable financial resolution that will not adversely affect the evaluation.

**Illustrative Case**  A university research group submitted a proposal to a federal agency for a regional evaluation of the effectiveness of representative community members as teacher aides. The evaluation was approved by an initial review panel. When the prospective funding agency reviewed the proposal for final approval, it was noted that the evaluation would take place in areas with predominantly white schools. The director of the funding agency insisted that the number of schools in the evaluation be increased by 50%, so that schools with large numbers of minority students would be included. Because of the federal agency's shortage of funds, it was not possible to increase the budget, and the investigators accepted the expanded plan without a budgetary increase.

When the investigators began the evaluation, they soon realized that including the additional schools required considerably more travel funds than were in the budget. It was also necessary to increase salaries to provide qualified staff members of minority background in order to have a research team that could relate to all the schools involved. The evaluators made no attempt to obtain additional funding from the supporting agency or elsewhere and did not receive permission to transfer funds between categories. In order to make the necessary savings, they replaced the professional classroom observers that were part of the planned evaluation team with unpaid undergraduate students. Further, they cut back markedly on the evaluation instruments that were to be used to measure student performance.

At the end of the first year of the project, the evaluators submitted a fiscal report that was superficially reviewed by the university fiscal officer and transmitted to the funding agency. The agency noted that funds had not been expended in accordance with the approved contract and immediately suspended support for the evaluation. The suspension continued for six months while new budget categories and an increased budget were negotiated. During this period, however, two of the five senior members of the evaluation team who were fully supported by the evaluation obtained employment elsewhere. The evaluation suffered considerably in rigor and definitiveness because of the staff turnover and activity delays.

**Analysis of the Case**   The evaluators should have anticipated the evaluation design elements that would become problematical during the evaluation and provided for them in the basic contract. Having failed to do this, however, the evaluators should have taken the matter up with the client as soon as it became apparent. At that time, the evaluators might have negotiated an appropriate change in the agreement. On the other hand, if the client would not agree to the change, the evaluators could have made the problem and their efforts a matter of record and proceeded with the original evaluation design to the best of their ability or could have withdrawn from the project.

# D
# ACCURACY STANDARDS

## SUMMARY OF THE STANDARDS

### D  Accuracy Standards

The Accuracy Standards are intended to ensure that an evaluation will reveal and convey technically adequate information about the features of the object being studied that determine its worth or merit. These standards are:

### D1  Object Identification

The object of the evaluation (program, project, material) should be sufficiently examined, so that the form(s) of the object being considered in the evaluation can be clearly identified.

### D2  Context Analysis

The context in which the program, project, or material exists should be examined in enough detail, so that its likely influences on the object can be identified.

### D3  Described Purposes and Procedures

The purposes and procedures of the evaluation should be monitored and described in enough detail, so that they can be identified and assessed.

### D4   Defensible Information Sources

The sources of information should be described in enough detail, so that the adequacy of the information can be assessed.

### D5   Valid Measurement

The information-gathering instruments and procedures should be chosen or developed and then implemented in ways that will assure that the interpretation arrived at is valid for the given use.

### D6   Reliable Measurement

The information-gathering instruments and procedures should be chosen or developed and then implemented in ways that will assure that the information obtained is sufficiently reliable for the intended use.

### D7   Systematic Data Control

The data collected, processed, and reported in an evaluation should be reviewed and corrected, so that the results of the evaluation will not be flawed.

### D8   Analysis of Quantitative Information

Quantitative information in an evaluation should be appropriately and systematically analyzed to ensure supportable interpretations.

### D9   Analysis of Qualitative Information

Qualitative information in an evaluation should be appropriately and systematically analyzed to ensure supportable interpretations.

### D10   Justified Conclusions

The conclusions reached in an evaluation should be explicitly justified, so that the audiences can assess them.

### D11   Objective Reporting

The evaluation procedures should provide safeguards to protect the evaluation findings and reports against distortion by the personal feelings and biases of any party to the evaluation.

# D1 OBJECT IDENTIFICATION

**Standard**  The object of the evaluation (program, project, material) should be sufficiently examined, so that the form(s) of the object being considered in the evaluation can be clearly identified.

**Overview**  The object of an evaluation is the particular thing under study. For the purposes of the Standards it is a program, a project, or an instructional material. It might also be a particular technique or practice used in a program or project. And it could include multiple versions of the particular thing being evaluated.

It is important to study the use of the object over time in order to avoid false impressions that the object is stable and does not change. This ongoing examination of the object(s) can help the evaluators to design, conduct, and report the evaluation. A valid characterization of the object(s) in interim and final reports will help the audience know each object's unique features and enable knowledgeable comparisons with similar objects. Finally, a description will help the audience associate each object's features with its effects and provide a helpful basis for further evaluations of the object should they be desired.

**Guidelines**  A. Ask the client and the other audience(s) to describe—orally, and, if possible, in writing—the object of the evaluation realistically in regard to such items as personnel, cost, procedures, location, facilities, setting, objectives, and potential side effects.

B. Ask the client and audience(s) to check the factual accuracy of the recorded descriptions of both the intended and the actual object.

C. Collect available descriptions of the object, including proposals, public relations reports, slide-tape presentations, and staff progress (and final) reports.

D. If the budget permits, engage independent observers to describe the object.

E. As part of the ongoing evaluation process, maintain up-to-date descriptions of the object from different information sources (e.g., participant observers, minutes of staff meetings, and progress reports), giving particular attention to changes that occur.

F. Consider developing separate descriptions for each aspect of the object being studied, including the different programs, projects, and materials that are employed with each group of people in the evaluation.

G. Record the obtained descriptions in a technical report, paying special attention to any discrepancies between intended object characteristics and actual characteristics when implemented.

**Pitfalls**  A. Relying solely on the client's or the funding proposal's descriptions of the object

B. Failing to check the accuracy of the obtained descriptions of the object through direct examination or observation

C. Glossing over a description of the object by saying, for example, that "the treatment was all that occurred between times 1 and 2," without describing the actual events

**Caveats**  A. Avoid forcing too precise a description when the object is still being developed.

B. Avoid concentrating so much on describing the object that insufficient time can be devoted to assessing its strengths and weaknesses.

**Illustrative Case**  A school district contracted to have a tutorial program at the secondary level evaluated over a two-year period. The evaluators conducted a comparative study.

All secondary students were screened, by means of teacher judgments and grades in school subjects, to locate those students who needed help. The identified students were then randomly divided into a tutorial group and a control group (students who would receive no special tutoring but whose school performance would be monitored for comparison with that of the tutorial group).

The evaluators asked the secondary school principal to administer the Tutorial Program so that the students selected for this program were tutored throughout the two-year period. At the end of the two years, the evaluators gathered student grades and teacher judgments of student progress. This information was obtained for both the tutorial group and the control group.

The evaluators found "no significant differences." Grade point averages for students in both groups had improved considerably, but about equally. Also, the teachers in the program judged that most students in both groups still needed special remedial instructional assistance.

At no stage did the program staff or the evaluators clearly describe the special assistance that students in the tutorial group actually received. Nor did they describe the instructional experiences of the members of the control group.

The evaluators concluded that the Tutorial Program had not made any unique contributions to the educational development of the students and recommended that it be dropped.

After the report was released, an association of parents and teachers in the secondary school where the project was conducted sent a letter of protest to the superintendent. They charged that the evaluators' conclusions and recommendations were unwarranted. They stated that the progress in grade point averages for the tutorial group was evidence that the Tutorial Program was making a contribution. They asserted that the teachers' report that most students still needed special assistance was an indication that there was a continuing need for the program, not that it had failed. They further argued that the evaluators should not have expected the tutorial and control groups to differ in their educational gains; they claimed that their Association, in cooperation with the school principal, had gotten ex-teachers from the community to volunteer their services in tutoring those students who needed and wanted tutoring but were being denied participation in the Tutorial Program. Also, the PTA group questioned the overall validity of the evaluation, arguing that the evaluators obviously had not learned what actually took place in the program.

**Analysis of the Case**  The evaluators should have monitored both the tutorial and control programs throughout the two-year project. This was essential for testing their assumptions about differences between tutorial and control conditions, and such monitoring might have led them and their clients to adjust the purposes and procedures of the evaluation.

Even if the decision was not to change the original evaluation plan, the evaluators should have reported, along with their conclusions and recommendations, accurate descriptions of the tutorial services that were received by both the tutorial group and the control group. These descriptions would have provided a basis for describing what activities made up the Tutorial Program and how much time and resources were devoted to them. The descriptions would have aided the evaluators and their audience to assess whether this program was well implemented, whether it provided tutorial services to students in the tutorial group beyond those provided to the control group, and whether the lack of differences in the educational gains for the tutorial and control groups could be explained by a lack of differences in the amounts and kinds of remedial tutorial services that these two groups received. Finally, if a competing program was discovered to be providing tutorial service to the control group, the evaluators might have studied it to determine its effectiveness, practicality, and costs relative to those of the Tutorial Program.

The evaluators could have done a number of things to obtain adequate descriptions of the Tutorial Program and the tutoring that was provided to members of the control group. At different times during the two years they could have asked the superintendent, the school principal, and selected teachers to give oral descriptions of the Tutorial Program and tutorial services being provided to the control group. The evaluators could have tape-recorded and transcribed these descriptions for future reference. They might have maintained case histories of the tutorial experiences of selected students in both groups. Classroom observations and interviews with teachers, students, and parents could have added to the evaluators' understanding of how the Tutorial Program operated and whether it differed much from the instructional services received by students in the control group. The evaluators could have incorporated the descriptions obtained by all these procedures into their report and used them in reaching conclusions.

# D2 CONTEXT ANALYSIS

**Standard** The context in which the program, project, or material exists should be examined in enough detail, so that its likely influences on the object can be identified.

**Overview** The context in which the object of an evaluation exists is the combination of the conditions surrounding the object that may influence its functioning. These conditions include the geographic location of the object, its timing, the political and social climate in the region at that time, relevant professional activities in progress, the nature of the staff, and pertinent economic conditions.

These and other contextual factors must be examined to assure that the evaluation can be designed, conducted, and reported in relation to them. Maintaining an understanding of the context is necessary if the evaluation is to be designed and carried out realistically and responsively.

Also, contextual information is needed to help the audiences interpret the evaluation. For example, the audience(s) would want to know whether a project's success or failure had been influenced by such things as improverished economic conditions; a divisive relationship between teachers and school administrators; parental support, apathy, or resistance; or a community-wide project to promote cultural opportunities.

Explication of the contextual conditions should aid the audience(s) to judge whether the context for the study is similar to other contexts in which the findings might be applied. Moreover, it should help the evaluators avoid claiming broader applicability of the findings than the context justifies.

This standard sometimes has implications for choosing where and when to conduct the evaluation. If evaluators have any options, they should select a context that is most like the contexts where the object being evaluated might be adopted.

**Guidelines**    A. Describe the object's social, political, and economic context using multiple sources (logs, records, demographic studies, newspaper clippings, legislative bills, etc.).

B. Maintain a log of unusual circumstances—such as a strike, a student protest, the passing of a millage increase, a snowstorm, etc.—that might have influenced the findings.

C. Record instances in which individuals, intentionally or otherwise, interfered with the object or gave special assistance.

D. In evaluations intended to service dissemination and adoption decisions, analyze how the object's context is similar to and different from selected contexts where the object might be adopted; and report significant contextual factors that are of interest to potential adopters (including educational administrators, teachers, students, parents, and other potentially interested groups).

**Pitfalls**    A. Viewing the object's context too narrowly and ignoring potentially important influences, such as political pressures or the restrictive influences of inadequate physical space

B. Accepting public relations documents as adequate descriptions of the context

**Caveat**    A. Avoid concentrating so much on analyzing the object's context that not enough time can be devoted to assessing its effectiveness.

**Illustrative Case**    A state education agency formed a panel of evaluators to evaluate a group of innovative public school projects which the agency had sponsored. The various projects were assigned to members of the panel. The panel members were expected to evaluate one project each within two months and report back to the agency.

One of the projects to be evaluated was in a secondary school of approximately 1,500 students and 90 faculty. A computer and terminals were the center of the innovation. A mathematics teacher was the chief developer and the purpose of the project was to familiarize students and faculty with programming and the many functions of computers.

While the computer had been installed for six months, the first terminal was available for only the last month. During the six-month period, some unique conditions and unusual events prevailed: the school was heavily engaged in the school district's campaign to pass a school tax issue; and the previous principal was replaced by one who had come from being principal of a school one-tenth the size of his present one. The evaluator's report to the state education department stated that the project was not achieving its purpose. This judgment was based on evidence that in six months only eight students and one faculty member had been involved in the project. There was no attempt to interpret this finding in light of the many contextual factors that may have influenced the result.

**Analysis of the Case**     The evaluator might have compiled a file of information about the conditions and events in the school, school district, and community during the life of the project. Using this file, the evaluator then could have prepared a report describing the details of the availability of terminals, the school's involvement in the tax election, and the change in principals during the introductory period of the innovative program. These contextual influences would have placed in perspective the low faculty involvement and other factors associated with the program.

The report to the state education department then could have taken into account that a context was required in which the faculty could devote more time than the tax election campaign had permitted, and when all equipment was available and use was encouraged.

By considering these contextual factors, the evaluator probably would have been led to present constructive feedback, not simply negative judgment.

# D3 DESCRIBED PURPOSES AND PROCEDURES

**Standard**  The purposes and procedures of the evaluation should be monitored and described in enough detail, so that they can be identified and assessed.

**Overview**  The purposes of an evaluation include its objectives (e.g., to judge the relative merits of competing textbooks, or to monitor and report on how well a project plan is implemented) and its intended uses (e.g., to help teachers choose a textbook or to help a school district carry out a special project). The procedures of an evaluation include the various ways in which information is gathered, organized, analyzed, and reported.

Since differences of opinion sometimes occur on what an evaluation's purposes and procedures should be (or actually were), the areas of agreement and disagreement need to be identified and assessed. Minimally, evaluators and clients at the outset of an evaluation should record their agreements about its purposes and procedures. To introduce greater objectivity than either of these sources can provide, it is also desirable (when feasible and especially in large-scale evaluations) to have independent evaluators monitor, describe, and judge the evaluation. Only when varying descriptions and judgments are obtained can underlying disagreements be reconciled or, at least, taken into account in interpreting findings.

Moreover, an evaluation's purposes and procedures should be clarified and recorded at different stages. These descriptions should occur at the beginning of the evaluation—at least in general terms—so that all participants will know what they are expected to do. Purposes and procedures should also be described periodically during the evaluation to provide a realistic view of (1) the appropriateness of the original plans and the extent to which they were implemented, or (2) how purposes and procedures were developed during the evaluation. At the conclusion of the evaluation, the audiences will need an up-to-date description of what the evaluators did and with what intent, so that the findings and recommendations can be judged and interpreted accordingly.

Such descriptions also have a number of other uses. They provide vital information to anyone who needs to evaluate the evaluation. They give other evaluators ideas and guidelines about how they might conduct similar evaluations in other settings. They define what purposes and procedures would have to be observed in replicating the evaluation. They can aid substantially in the dissemination of the techniques that were employed in the evaluation. And the descriptions of evaluation purposes and procedures can constitute good case materials for use in instructing evaluators.

**Guidelines** A. Record the client's initial conceptions of the purpose of the evaluation.

B. Record the client's initial conceptions of how the evaluation's purposes will be achieved.

C. Keep a copy of the evaluation plan and the evaluation contract (if one was negotiated).

D. Keep field notes on actual implementation procedures.

E. Reach a clear understanding with the client of major changes in evaluation purposes and procedures as the changes are made.

F. Record any major changes in purposes and procedures.

G. Preserve and make available for responsibly planned reviews and further analyses, data (unless legal or contractual stipulations forbid doing so), field procedures for collecting data, and records of analysis procedures.

H. At the conclusion of the evaluation, compile both a summary and a full technical report on what its purposes were and how it was conducted.

I. Whenever feasible, and especially in large-scale evaluations, engage independent evaluators to review and evaluate purposes and procedures of evaluations.

**Pitfalls**  A. Assuming that a funding proposal sufficiently describes an evaluation's actual purposes and procedures

B. Assuming that the purposes and procedures agreed to by the client and the evaluator at the outset of an evaluation will remain unchanged and be adhered to during the evaluation

**Caveats**  A. Do not insist on an extensive definition of an evaluation's purposes and procedures at the outset if such an early definition would prevent a flexible approach when one is indicated (as, for example, in an evaluation designed to aid in the invention and development of new strategies for integrating school districts); if such early definitions subsequently contradict the evaluation approach being followed (e.g., a case study of a school district's efforts to deliver educational services when school buildings are closed because of an energy crisis); or if such early definitions would unduly restrict the collection of outcome information (e.g., concentrating on outcomes that pertain to objectives and paying little attention to possible side effects).

B. Do not conclude that purposes and procedures are sound simply because they are carefully described.

**Illustrative Case**  An independent study teaching approach was under consideration for a district's high school mathematics program. Before adopting the program on a district-wide basis, the assistant superintendent of instruction decided that the approach should be evaluated in competition with the district's regular classroom instruction approach.

The assistant superintendent and the district's evaluation staff arrived at a written formal agreement including the following:

1. The purpose of the evaluation was to help the high school mathematics department decide whether to adopt the independent study approach.

2. The procedures were to conduct a district-wide comparison of the two approaches, involving twenty percent of the district's high school mathematics teachers selected randomly and all the students enrolled in their classes.

3. Mathematics achievement, student attitude, and teacher enthusiasm were to be assessed at the end of each year.

4. Teachers were to be chosen and assigned randomly to the two different approaches.

The assistant superintendent subsequently decided that the purpose of the evaluation should be narrowed to serve mainly as feedback for strengthening the program in the experimental state rather than for decision-making on school-wide adoption. She also changed the procedure for assigning teachers and students to the project which resulted in their not being randomly assigned.

The evaluator, assuming that the evaluation purposes and procedures, once agreed upon, would remain constant, collected and analyzed the data as originally planned and reported the findings. He found that students' attitudes toward the approaches remained about the same, but student achievement as well as the teachers' enthusiasm was significantly greater for the independent study approach. The report judged this approach superior and recommended it for adoption.

The assistant superintendent expressed disappointment that the report did not provide adequate direction for improving the independent study approach. And teachers complained that the findings were not dependable, first, because in many cases teachers who were assigned to the independent study approach were biased in favor of it before the study began, and, second, the students in independent study classes were generally high achievers prior to entering the program.

**Analysis of the Case**  The evaluator should not have assumed that purposes and procedures, once agreed upon, would remain constant throughout the project. He therefore should have taken steps to monitor and record changes in purpose and procedures as they occurred.

Periodically, he might have met with the assistant superintendent to review purposes and to check on the implementation of those procedures which were not directly under his control.

Finally, near the end of the evaluation, he could have met with the assistant superintendent and others involved in the procedural aspects of the evaluation in order to consider the full description of the evaluation's evolved purposes and procedures in preparation for formulating his conclusions and recommendations.

# D4 DEFENSIBLE INFORMATION SOURCES

**Standard**   The sources of information should be described in enough detail, so that the adequacy of the information can be assessed.

**Overview**   There are many sources of information in an evaluation study. These include individual persons and groups, documents and films, audio and visual tapes, and the like.

It is important to select a variety of sources, so that the information they yield can be compared. For example, test scores for a class may take on added meaning if accompanied by a qualitative account of what was happening in the classroom.

These sources can be tapped in many different ways. The people and groups can be tested, surveyed, observed, and interviewed. The documents, films, and tapes can be content-analyzed and described. And situations can be observed and reported.

In choosing sources and ways of using them, evaluators can usually expect to obtain only a portion of the available, useful information. For example, normally they cannot test, interview, survey, or observe everyone who is in the population of interest. They must select samples of such sources. These may be drawn according to some formal procedure as by random sampling, or they may be drawn selectively (as in the use of intact classroom groups or volunteers). Moreover, the samples may remain relatively stable during the evaluation or they may change considerably.

Evaluators should document and report their information sources, the criteria and methods used to select them, the means used to derive information from them, how they were selected as samples of some larger population of interest, and any unique and biasing features of the obtained information.

These descriptions should be sufficient to permit others to determine the adequacy of the sources for addressing the evaluative questions. Poorly described information sources can reduce an evaluation's credibility. They can also mislead members of the audience to assume that the evaluation's conclusions and recommendations are based on sound information, even when this is not true.

**Guidelines** A. Describe the sources of information (e.g., 100 individuals, 12 classrooms, 16 institutions, 12 occasions, 30 one-hour audio tapes) that were used in the particular study.

B. Document the process (e.g., the interview, content analysis, or test) by which information was collected from each source, and retain copies of the information-gathering instruments for inclusion in a technical appendix.

C. For each source, document the sampling procedure that was used, including a definition of the population (e.g., the third graders in a given school during a given year) and how the particular sources were chosen (e.g., through drawing a 10% random sample).

D. In the cases of prespecified samples of human subjects, document the attrition during the study and the contributing factors (e.g., volunteer subjects or a transient student population), and assess whether the dropouts were different, in any respects, from those subjects that remained.

E. In cases where information was collected through an iterative, developmental process instead of according to a fully specified plan, indicate the rules (such as redundancy or marginal returns) by which decisions not to collect further information were made.

F. Whenever possible use pertinent previously collected information.

G. Project the data sources, sampling procedure, data collection process, and use of pertinent prior information in the plan for the evaluation; include descriptions of actual information and sources and copies of data-gathering instruments and procedures in a technical appendix to the final evaluation report; and assess the adequacy of the information sources in the body of the final evaluation report.

**Pitfalls**    A. Labeling information sources (e.g., fourth-grade students) but not describing them

B. Assuming without supporting evidence that different information sources (e.g., progress reports prepared by a project's staff vs. those prepared by the school district's evaluation office) are equally adequate

C. Labeling information sources as adequate or inadequate and discarding the latter, since all information sources are only partially adequate

**Caveats**    A. Avoid the assumption that information based on interviews, testimony, etc., is nonobjective and hence not worthly of consideration. Objectivity is a relative matter to be assessed in terms of the expert knowledge which respondents bring to the evaluation, the extent to which they are committed to a particular point of view, and the relationship of the person collecting the information to the object or the information sources (see D11, Objective Reporting).

B. Avoid concentrating so much on documenting and assessing the appropriateness of the information sources that insufficient time can be devoted to gathering and using information or that the main message is obscured by the documentation. Often general accounts and assessments are sufficient.

**Illustrative Case**    An evaluator was called upon by the chairperson of a state's board of higher education to evaluate a controversial teacher education program designed specifically to provide graduates suited for teaching in open area classrooms in the state. The purpose of the evaluation was to supply information relevant to future allocation of funds to the program.

The evaluator launched an extensive data collection effort, including: questionnaires sent to superintendents, principals, and students; and interviews with the program director, her staff, recent graduates, and students still in the program. While the response rates were low the data from these sources generally showed the program to be successful, and the evaluator's report influenced the board's decision to continue the program.

However, critics of the program in the state legislature attacked the report. They charged that the evaluation was inconclusive because the samples of respondents were insufficiently described to assure that the results reflected accurately the population of which they were a part. The critics questioned the credibility of information because response rates were low, and because no checks had been made to determine the comparability of respondents and nonrespondents. Also, it was charged that the recent graduates surveyed had been chosen because of their positive feelings toward the program.

Board members, smarting under the critics' attack, refused to reverse their decision publicly but failed to allocate funds at the level previously determined. Further evaluations were not commissioned; and, at a subsequent board meeting, the program was terminated.

**Analysis of the Case**     The evaluator might have carefully described each sample and the procedures used to choose the sample and assure that it was representative of the population from which it was chosen. In each survey, the evaluator should have checked whether those who did not respond to the survey were in some way different from those who did. This could have been done by choosing a random sample of both groups—those who responded, and those who did not—and seeing whether they were different with respect to certain variables which might bias their responses. Having done this, the evaluator could have reported whether or not he had found differences between the two groups which might influence their responses; he could then have determined whether the respondents could be considered as representative.

# D5 VALID MEASUREMENT

**Standard**    The information-gathering instruments and procedures should be chosen or developed and then implemented in ways that will assure that the interpretation arrived at is valid for the given use.

**Overview**    Measurement validity concerns the soundness of the inferences that are made from the results of the data-gathering process. Validation is the process of compiling evidence that supports the use and the interpretations to be made of a given measurement device or procedure. No simple prescription can be given for success in this process.

In general, the validation process should include the following elements:

1. a detailed description of content and constructs to be measured;

2. an analysis of what a particular instrument or procedure purports to measure;

3. a detailed description of how the instrument or procedure is administered, scored, and interpreted in the particular evaluation;

4. a presentation of evidence—both qualitative and quantitative—that indicates whether the use of the particular instrument or procedure is justified; and,

5. an overall assessment of the validity of the use and interpretation of the instrument or procedure.

It is clear from the preceding elements that validity is not a property inherent in a measurement instrument or procedure, and separate from the questions being addressed. Thus, it is insufficient to say that an instrument or procedure is valid because a publisher or researcher has reported favorable results from a study of its validity. The validity of a measurement instrument or procedure depends specifically on how it is used, the questions being addressed, the conditions of data collection, the characteristics of the persons who provide the data, and, especially, the interpretation of the results.

It is highly desirable that evaluators measure multiple outcomes and use multiple data-gathering instruments and procedures—including questionnaires, interviews, rating forms, observations, tests, and descriptions. All of the measures used must be validated, singly and in combination, to ensure that they will answer effectively the evaluation's questions.

One major reason for using multiple measures is to assure that the full range of important variables is assessed. No program, project, or material can be adequately characterized and assessed by reference to a single variable. Many kinds of variables—such as attitudes, achievements, costs, and use of time—typically need to be considered, and this fact dictates the use of multiple measures.

A different but equally important reason for using multiple measures is that any one measure of a given variable is fallible. Whenever practicable, evaluators should use several methods of assessment in combination to get a better reading on a single variable. For example, conclusions regarding student achievement in working with fractions have greater validity if results are obtained both by a multiple choice test which allows coverage of many exercises in a given time and by a completion test in which the students have to find the answers for themselves.

Validity is the most fundamental concern in the use of any measurement process. It matters little how reliably something is measured if it results in the wrong inferences.

**Guidelines**  A. Check measurement instruments and procedures against the objectives and content of the program being evaluated, and, whenever possible, obtain judgments of the instruments and procedures from teachers and others involved in the program.

B. Report in detail the reasons for selecting each measurement instrument and procedure, and highlight the evidence that supports the uses of the instrument.

C. Be especially careful when collecting opinions to consider whether the respondents are motivated to tell the truth and to make certain that the way the questions are worded does not unduly affect the results.

D. Be especially careful when using newly developed instruments, and present the rationale for the type and extent of validity claimed.

E. Assess the validity of the total set of measurement instruments and procedures used in relation to all the questions being addressed by the evaluation.

F. In reporting evaluation findings, point out common misinterpretations of a measure or score that a reader is likely to make.

**Pitfall**
A. Accepting a measuring instrument for its general characteristics (e.g., title, format, and reputation) rather than its applicability to the construct being measured

**Caveats**
A. Do not rule out the exploratory use of data-gathering instruments with little or no evidence of validity. When time, resources, and available data-gathering instruments will not permit complete validation beforehand, or even after completion of the evaluation, evaluators are advised to:

point out that these instruments are exploratory;

report that results must be interpreted with caution and within strictly defined limits of context, group, and other characteristics relevant to the object of the evaluation;

report the extent to which program staff were involved in developing or choosing instruments.

B. Use multiple measures to accomplish a valid assessment, but do so in as nondisruptive and parsimonious a manner as possible. Often it is desirable to employ nonreactive measures and to assess samples instead of populations; it is always good to search for pertinent existing records (see B3, Cost Effectiveness).

**Illustrative Case**
Units on ecology were introduced for the first time in all grades in a middle school. The school's curriculum committee re-

quested that the school district's evaluation department evaluate the effectiveness of these units. Specifically, the committee wanted to know whether the students who had completed the units had increased their knowledge about environmental issues (e.g., preservation of endangered species and conservation of scarce resources) and whether they had decreased their practice of littering the school grounds.

The evaluators administered a test and a questionnaire to the students before they took the ecology units and after they had completed these units. The test was the science subtest of a national standardized achievement test, including hygiene, biology, and earth science. The questionnaire was a self-report instrument that asked the students to rate themselves and their classmates on factors related to school citizenship. This questionnaire included items on respect for other students, respect for teachers, and respect for school property. Following the collection and analysis of data, the evaluators reported that there was no change from preinstruction to postinstruction scores on two parallel forms of the subtest. They reported further that the students' scores on the citizenship questionnaire did not change following instruction. The curriculum committee expressed disappointment in the evaluation, pointing out that it really did not answer their questions.

**Analysis of the Case**  The evaluators should have chosen or developed data-gathering instruments and procedures that responded directly to the curriculum committee's questions. The evaluators could have checked these instruments and procedures against the content and objectives of the ecology unit. They could have gotten the curriculum committee and the middle school teachers to offer judgments about whether the instruments and procedures would adequately address their questions. The evaluators could have observed the ecology units in operation and also observed the students in and out of school during the time they were enrolled in the ecology units to discover possible unintended effects of the units on the students' behavior. The evaluators might have collected data on the quantity of wastepaper, bottles, and cans found in specific locations around the school plant, the extent to which students used both sides of notebook paper, and so on.

# D6 RELIABLE MEASUREMENT

**Standard**  The information-gathering instruments and procedures should be chosen or developed and then implemented in ways that will assure that the information obtained is sufficiently reliable for the intended use.

**Overview**  A reliable measure is one that provides consistent indications of the characteristic being investigated.

To obtain dependable results efficiently, evaluators should choose instruments that have acceptable reliability for their intended uses. Also, they should check and report the reliability of their measures as they are actually used in the evaluation.

Any data-gathering instrument or procedure is susceptible to many sources of error which, from time to time, cause fluctuations in the results from one source of information to another, or from one part of a measure to another. Because there are different sources of error, there are a variety of procedures for estimating reliability.

The specific reliability concerns relevant to an evaluation will vary according to different types and uses of information. In some instances, the primary concern may be with stability; that is, the results should not be unique to a particular moment or occasion, to a particular day of the week or time of day. In other situations, the concern may be with the equivalence of the results obtained on one form of a test versus an alternate form or with the consistency of ratings obtained from different raters.

In many evaluations, the most important type of reliability involves the reliability of the average score of a group, instead of the reliability of scores for individuals. In this situation, the traditional methods used to estimate reliability can be misleading because they reflect only the reliability of the between-person rankings. This traditional type of reliability coefficient may be low, without necessarily producing any great difficulty when the evaluator is mainly concerned with group means. Then it is the measurement error associated with the mean that provides the proper reliability index, instead of the typically much larger error associated with individual scores. Thus, in such cases the reliability of group means should be examined directly.

**Guidelines**    A. Collect reliability information which is directly relevant to the ways in which the measuring instruments or observation techniques will be used in the evaluation.

**Pitfalls**    A. Interpreting evidence of one type of reliability (e.g., internal consistency, stability over time, inter-observer agreement) as evidence of any other type

B. Depending upon reliability results reported for a published instrument without considering the likely effects of differences in setting and sample

C. Interpreting a low traditional reliability coefficient for a test as an indication that the test will necessarily provide unreliable or invalid average scores for groups

D. Failing to take into account that the reliability of a test will fluctuate depending on how, when, and to whom it is administered

E. Deciding not to use a measurement technique to reflect group differences because there are no existing traditional reliability data

F. Considering a traditional reliability coefficient as necessarily reflecting upon the degree to which a mastery test reliably discriminates between mastery and nonmastery

**Caveats**    A. Expect that the most that can reasonably be achieved in many evaluations is that the measurement techniques are (a) administered so as to minimize unreliability, (b) described so that others may make their own judgments regarding reliability, and (c) defended indirectly regarding reliability by provision of evidence about their validity.

B. It is frequently found that differences between scores obtained for an individual at two points in time are less reliable than either of the two scores.

**Illustrative Case**    Evaluators constructed an observation checklist and two forms of each of several objectives-referenced tests for use in evaluating an innovative instructional technique. The objectives-referenced tests each contained ten objectives with five items per objective.

The evaluators pretested their tests by administering one form of each test on one occasion to classes at grades two and four in a pilot sample of six schools. They used a standard formula to compute an internal consistency coefficient for the total score based on 50 items (10 objectives with five questions each) for each form of the test. Since the internal consistency of each form was greater than .80 the test forms were judged to be sufficiently reliable.

A single observer was sent out to observe the same classroom at each of the six schools twice. An interval of three weeks separated the first and second observations. Correlations between the first and second observation results were computed for each item on the checklist with the result that no correlation was below .61.

Based on these activities, the evaluators concluded that their tests and observation checklist were sufficiently reliable for use in the evaluation. However, this conclusion was later attacked. A group of teachers who participated in the evaluation charged that the different forms of the tests were not equivalent and that they yielded unfair comparisons of classrooms and of schools. They said they couldn't see the point of assessing the reliability of each test as a whole, since the tests were constructed to yield subscores for specific objectives. They also expressed doubt that all the items assigned to each objective were consistent measures of the objective. Moreover, they charged that the results of the observations were more a function of who did each one than of what was happening in the classroom. The evaluators were unable to defend themselves against these charges.

**Analysis of the Case**    Both forms of each test might have been pretested by administering them to a single sample of students on two occasions. This would have allowed an estimate of the consistency of the results from one form to the other for each objective as well as for the total scores for the ten objectives combined. Since the tests had been developed to determine whether certain instructional objectives had been achieved, the percentages of students who were identified by both forms of the test as achieving or failing each objective would have given appropriate indices of reliability of the equivalence of the forms.

The observation checklist and procedures might have been pretested by having two or more different observers make the observations independently but simultaneously. The percentage of inter-observer agreements could have been calculated as an index of the reliability of each item on the checklist. Through this procedure the evaluators could have ascertained whether consistent results could be gotten by different observers using the same form.

Overall, the evaluators should have been more discriminating in choosing the types of reliability that were most appropriate to their evaluation. They should not have made the common error of treating internal consistency and test-retest reliability as the only ways of assessing reliability.

# D7 SYSTEMATIC DATA CONTROL

**Standard**  The data collected, processed, and reported in an evaluation should be reviewed and corrected, so that the results of the evaluation will not be flawed.

**Overview**  Systematic data control implies that steps will be taken to assure that all data used will be as error-free as is humanly possible.

There are many possibilities for error in collecting, scoring, recording, coding, filing, collating, and analyzing data. The evaluators may fail to administer an instrument to the intended group of respondents. Respondents may make errors on a paper and pencil test because the directions were unclear or because intended administration procedures were not followed. Keypunch operators may misread data sheets or punch the wrong key on their machines. Clerical personnel may lose data sheets by misfiling them. Test scorers may use the wrong key to score a test. Data analysts may use the wrong formula or make arithmetic errors. Or, evaluators may summarize or report findings incorrectly. These are but a few of the ways that avoidable errors may become part of an evaluation's data base and findings.

Evaluators should eliminate as many of these errors as possible. Their unchecked presence in an evaluation can lead to erroneous conclusions and recommendations, which, in turn, can result in misguided actions. Also, if errors are detected in the evaluation procedures or report which the evaluators had not attempted to search out and correct, the total evaluation effort might be discredited or rendered vulnerable.

Evaluators should not assume that even highly qualified and dedicated persons will not make clerical-type errors or that they will fully monitor their own work. A safer assumption is that anything that can go wrong probably will. It is, therefore, prudent to institute a systematic program of training, controls, and accuracy checks.

**Guidelines**   A. Take whatever steps are necessary to ensure that participants in the evaluation are adequately oriented and trained to carry out their roles and that they are sensitized to the kinds of mistakes that they should be careful to avoid.

B. Allow sufficient time to gather and consider all the needed data.

C. Maintain control of the original data throughout the study, especially when data processing has been delegated to individuals or agencies not under the direct control of the evaluators.

D. Adopt and implement standard procedures for storing and retrieving data.

E. Implement systematic checks for errors in the collecting, processing, and reporting of data.

**Pitfalls**   A. Failing to have keypunched data verified for accuracy

B. Assuming that test-scoring machines and computers give consistently reliable results

C. Failing to ensure that a computer program accurately reflects the intended formulas

D. Assuming that people who administer standardized tests follow the procedures outlined in the publisher's manual

E. Assuming that respondents read, understand, and follow all directions they are given

**Caveat**   A. Expect that even data which are carefully checked and re-checked are likely to have a few errors. The important consideration is that the rate of error be kept under control.

**Illustrative Case**   A government agency announced their intention to provide $100,000 contracts to three school districts in each state for the purpose of field testing a nationally developed program in career education. The agency received many proposals and assigned four judges to rate each proposal on thirteen specified criteria. The agency then totaled and averaged the ratings of each. The ratings for the proposals from each state were then ranked from highest to lowest and contracts were awarded to the three school districts whose proposals had the highest overall ratings.

One group of proposal writers that had invested much time and effort in the development of their proposal was greatly surprised and disappointed when their school district was not awarded a contract. One member of this group traveled to Washington to obtain an explanation. She was even more disappointed when she learned from a government official that her district's proposal had been given a very low overall rating.

She could not accept this report and demanded an audit of the individual ratings that had been assigned to her district's proposal. The government official complied, and, much to his embarrassment, found that the overall rating had been calculated by dividing by six instead of four (judges). The corrected calculation revealed that the district's proposal should have received the highest overall rating of any proposal from that district's state. Moreover, a subsequent check of the overall ratings assigned to all the proposals submitted revealed five more cases of proposals rejected on the basis of averaging the totals by six instead of four judges.

**Analysis of the Case**    The officials of the government agency should have ensured that their funding decisions accurately reflected the collected judgments. They could have had their judges verify the accuracy of the ratings, calculations, and projected awards. They could have employed an independent evaluator to check and verify the accuracy of the entire process of collecting and analyzing judgments. And they could have had two staff members independently calculate the overall ratings for each proposal.

# D8 ANALYSIS OF QUANTITATIVE INFORMATION

**Standard**  Quantitative information in an evaluation should be appropriately and systematically analyzed to ensure supportable interpretations.

**Overview**  Quantitative information consists of facts and claims that are represented by numbers. Quantitative analysis is the process of compiling, organizing, manipulating, and validating such information so that certain questions about an object can be answered.

Many evaluations produce and analyze quantitative information of some sort, which may include, but is not limited to, the age and socioeconomic characteristics of students; measures of their achievement, attitudes, and behaviors; and measures of characteristics of the program, project, or instructional materials being evaluated. The task of quantitative analysis is to organize, summarize, interpret, and report these counts and measures so their meaning will be clear.

Evaluations often involve a comparison of different groups of students in different programs. The groups being compared are seldom formed by random assignment. Rather, they tend to be natural groupings which may differ in various ways prior to participation in the program being evaluated. Analytical methods that may be used to adjust for initial differences between groups require a variety of assumptions. Since it is difficult to check such assumptions, it is often advisable, when time and resource permit, to use several different methods of analysis involving different sets of assumptions to determine whether a replicable pattern of results was obtained.

Overall comparisons of average performance for groups receiving different programs are generally insufficient. Analyses of effects for various identifiable subgroups are also needed, because a program may have differential effects for various subgroups. Thus, a program that appears beneficial in terms of overall averages may actually be harmful for some subgroups. For example, materials that are useful for the child of average achievement may be dysfunctional for children with reading difficulties.

Many different conclusions can be supported through quantitative analysis and it is the responsibility of evaluators to assure that the use of such analytic methods is not leading them, or their audiences, to faulty conclusions. While there is no one best method for analyzing a given set of data, evaluators should ensure that they can rationally defend their methodology, the underlying assumptions, the calculations, and the conclusions.

**Guidelines**  A. Choose an analysis procedure that is appropriate to the evaluation's questions and quantitative information.

B. Report potential weaknesses in the data collection or analysis design—e.g., violation of assumptions—and describe their possible influence on conclusions.

C. When feasible, collect and analyze independent sets of data to bolster what might otherwise be a weak quantitative analysis.

**Pitfalls**  A. Allowing data collection and analysis considerations to reduce the questions under study to a false simplicity

B. Assuming that statistically significant results are always practically significant, and that statistically insignificant results are always practically insignificant

C. Testing students to select some of them for participation in an evaluation and then using their scores on the selection test along with their scores on a post-test to compute difference scores to be used as an index of change

D. Assuming that gain scores, matching, or analysis of covariance will always provide an adequate adjustment for initial differences between groups

E. Interpreting norms based on the performance of individual students as if they were norms based on group means

**Caveats**  A. Do not conclude that all evaluations need to use statistical analyses.

B. Do not conclude that all evaluations should be comparative experimental studies.

C. Do not use complex statistical techniques just to impress; often the audience can be better served by the use of simple techniques, such as graphs, frequency distributions, and scatter plots.

D. Do not overstress rigor at the expense of relevance.

**Illustrative Case**   A company contracted with a school to run a special five-week project for improving the reading skills of low achieving fourth-grade children. The school regularly administered a reading test to all students at the beginning of the year, and all who scored below a certain level were enrolled in the special project. A parallel form of this test was administered to the participants and nonparticipants at the conclusion of the five-week project.

The school's evaluator computed gain scores for each student and reported that the influence of the project on the participating students was consistently positive and substantial.

**Analysis of the Case**   This was a faulty conclusion. The gain scores of the participants probably would have been positive, on the average, even if the project had had no influence. Since the pre-test was imperfect, and the participants were chosen for their low scores, most students' scores would rise because of errors in their pre-test scores in the opposite direction. Such a rise in a group's average performance should not be mistaken for the effect of a project. More likely, it is the result of a statistical artifact called regression toward the mean, which results from using an imperfect test to select students.

This particular design could have been analyzed by fitting prediction equations to the pre-test and post-test data for the participant and the nonparticipant groups separately. Under certain conditions the project effect could have been estimated from the difference between the two regression lines produced by the equations.

# D9 ANALYSIS OF QUALITATIVE INFORMATION

**Standard**    Qualitative information in an evaluation should be appropriately and systematically analyzed to ensure supportable interpretations.

**Overview**    Qualitative information consists of facts and interpretations that are in narrative rather than numerical form. This information comes from many sources: structured and unstructured interviews, participant and nonparticipant observations, hearings, documents and records, and unobtrusive data collection procedures of various kinds. It may be gathered intentionally, or it may come to one's awareness quite unexpectedly. It may focus on decisions, objectives, plans, processes, outcomes, etc.; and it may be recorded as descriptions, logical arguments, interpretations, and impressions.

Qualitative analysis is the process of compiling, analyzing, and interpreting qualitative information about an object that will answer particular questions about that object. The result is a narrative presentation, in which numerical values are usually not assigned to any of the information. While qualitative data can often be quantitatively as well as qualitatively analyzed, qualitative analysis may give depth and perspective to the data that quantitative analysis alone may not be able to achieve.

An important distinction between qualitative and quantitative analysis is that for qualitative analysis the observation protocols, categories of information, and methods of summarization cannot all be predetermined. Qualitative analysis often involves an interactive and iterative process, whereby the evaluator returns to relevant audiences and data sources to confirm and/or expand the purposes of the evaluation and to test conclusions. It often requires an intuitive sifting of expressed concerns and relevant observations; it cannot always be accomplished by application of prespecified rules for data reduction. Therefore, the evaluator must assure the accuracy of findings by seeking confirmatory evidence from more than one source and by subjecting inferences to independent verification.

In general, qualitative information has been appropriately analyzed when: a set of categories has been derived that are necessary to account for the information that has been uncovered and sufficient to document, illuminate, and respond to the evaluation questions; the information classified into these categories as well as the categories themselves have been tested for validity and reliability; and the meaningfulness of derived conclusions and recommendations has been demonstrated by reference to those categories. As in quantitative analysis, the essence of this standard is the conscious effort to avoid faulty conclusions due to inappropriate analysis methods which may lead to premature closure or inadequate cross-checking of findings.

**Guidelines**  A. Choose an analysis procedure and method of summarization that is appropriate to the question with which the study is concerned and to the nature of the qualitative information.

B. Report potential weaknesses in the data collection or analysis design, e.g., single source information that seemed important but could not be cross-checked, or contradictory findings that could not be reconciled.

C. Establish meaningful categories of information—for example, parental support, home/career conflict, intrinsic rewards, and dominance—by identifying regular and recurrent data items. As much as possible, these categories should be internally consistent and mutually exclusive; and they should leave no apparent logical gaps. It is a good idea to have an expert in the area of study verify that the set of categories represents the data adequately and consistently.

D. Stop analyzing information when sources are exhausted, redundancy occurs, and/or extensive regularities are noted.

E. Test the consistency of findings by having two or more independent evaluators analyze the same set of information, or by having an expert external auditor verify that the data have been consistently analyzed.

F. Communicate frequently with representatives of the audiences to ensure that they find the qualitative analyses appropriate and the conclusions and recommendations meaningful.

**Pitfalls**  A. Regarding qualitative data analysis as relatively nonrigorous and as something that can be accomplished well enough on an intuitive basis

B. Failing to consider alternative interpretations of reality and/or multiple value perspectives that exist in the evaluation situation

C. Failing to differentiate different sources of qualitative information on such bases as credibility, degree of expertise, and degree of involvement

**Caveats**  A. Recognize the complementariness of qualitative and quantitative data and interpretations.

B. Do not concentrate so heavily on describing the unique feature of a situation that its generalizable features are not examined.

C. Do not overstress relevance at the expense of rigor.

D. Do not overstress the particularities of a situation at the expense of more general working hypotheses or inferences.

E. Avoid overresponding to emergent categories which, while interesting, are irrelevant to the questions that the data were collected to answer.

**Illustrative Case**  Two members of a school district's evaluation office were assigned by the school superintendent to help her analyze a set of qualitative information that had been gathered to evaluate a special crime prevention project in the district. The project had an emergent format, with the activities carried on within it changing over time as the staff gained insight and experience. The superintendent needed accurate information about the nature of the project activities at different times for inclusion in a progress report to the funding agency that was due in three months. That agency also wanted to know whether contacts between youngsters enrolled in the project and various law enforcement agencies—the police, the courts, and juvenile officers—had been reduced during the first operational year.

A considerable amount of information was available for analysis. Each staff member had kept a daily diary of project activities. Four times during the year, written and oral testimony had been received at hearings attended by students, teachers, counselors, parents, juvenile officers, health officials, and representatives of the business community. Staff members had maintained a file of pertinent newspaper clippings, and they had kept detailed case study records for a sample of ten youngsters. A community advisory council had met monthly to hear and discuss project progress reports, and minutes of the meetings had been maintained. School cumulative files for each enrolled youngster were also available, as were official records of police, court and juvenile probation officer contacts.

The evaluators spent more than a month getting acquainted with these materials and in perusing the contents. They developed a set of descriptive categories within which virtually every entry in the staff logs, hearings records, newspaper articles, case study records, and cumulative files could be classified. They also developed a frequency count for the number of times each enrolled youngster had had contact with a law enforcement agency during the first year of the project as well as in the immediately preceding year. Two things were immediately evident: (1) only a small proportion of the classified materials provided any insight into the nature of project activities and how they changed over the year, and (2) the number of law enforcement agency contacts was virtually identical in each of the two examined years. The evaluators, running out of time, were able to provide only sketchy accounts of activities, and informed the superintendent that the project had proved unsuccessful in reducing law enforcement agency contacts. When the superintendent reported these findings to the funding agency, support was withdrawn and the project was aborted.

Project staff were stunned by this development, especially because the count of contacts had weighed so heavily in the decision. They pointed out that during the first examined years (the preproject year), these contacts primarily took the form of arrests and court appearances for trial, while during the second examined year (the first project year), these contacts were primarily supervisory and counseling sessions with juvenile officers. The latter group declared that they had in fact been well pleased with the changes they were witnessing in the enrolled youngsters' attitudes and demeanor.

**Analysis of the Case**  The evaluators carrying out this analysis made two fundamental errors. First, they failed to recognize the need to bound their inquiry and so wasted a great deal of time in organizing data irrelevant to their purposes. Qualitative inquiry must, no less than quantitative inquiry, be guided. Second, they permitted frequency counts to substitute for an adequate analysis of the nature of the contacts between enrolled youngsters and law enforcement agencies. The evaluators should have attended first to the questions that they needed to answer. They should have entered only those records most likely to furnish the information they sought, e.g., staff logs to answer the question of what sorts of activities were mounted and how they changed over the year. They should have been less hasty in converting contact records to numbers which failed to reflect differences in kinds of contacts. Even the most cursory thought about the kinds of contacts being recorded should have led the evaluators to read the records classifying those contacts, an effort which, had they engaged in it, would have quickly led them to a very different conclusion about the project's effectiveness.

# D10 JUSTIFIED CONCLUSIONS

**Standard**  The conclusions reached in an evaluation should be explicitly justified, so that the audiences can assess them.

**Overview**  The conclusions of an evaluation, which represent judgments and recommendations, must be defensible and defended. To be defensible, conclusions must be based on sound logic and appropriate information. To be sufficiently defended, they must be reported along with an account of the evaluation's procedures, information, and underlying assumptions, and with a discussion of possible alternative explanations of the findings and why they were rejected.

This standard is important for at least two reasons. Unverified conclusions may be faulty, leading the audience to inappropriate actions. And, the conclusions may be disregarded, whatever their merits, if the audience does not receive sufficient information for determining whether they are warranted.

**Guidelines**  A. Develop conclusions that both respond to the audience's questions and faithfully reflect the evaluation's procedures and findings.

B. Search out, use, and report pertinent prior information that aids in developing relevant, justifiable conclusions (see D5, Valid Measurement).

C. Whenever possible, generate, assess, and report plausible alternative explanations of the findings.

D. Advise the audience to be cautious in interpreting equivocal findings in the evaluation report.

**Pitfalls**  A. Concentrating on answering the audience's questions without taking appropriate account of the limitations of the evaluation's procedures and findings

B. Ignoring possible side effects in reaching conclusions about the effectiveness of the object of the evaluation

C. Basing conclusions on a single source of information, a single type of data (such as students' test scores), or a single analytic technique

**Caveats**  A. Do not become so cautious in interpreting the findings of an evaluation that the audience's questions are not addressed.

B. Do not abstain from reporting hunches, estimates, and interpretations that may not be borne out by the data, but clearly label these as such.

**Illustrative Case**  An evaluation firm contracted to field-test a federally financed K-12 program in ecological education. The field test was to take place in three urban, four suburban, and ten rural school districts.

Officials of the government agency that financed the program's development wanted to know whether it was sufficiently meritorious to warrant widespread dissemination. Specifically, they wanted to know whether students participating in this program would achieve its objectives, whether teachers using the program would incorporate its ideas on ecology into their existing courses, and how a sample of curriculum specialists would rate the program against other approaches to ecological education.

A representative of the government agency suggested that the evaluators review the report from the pilot test of the program. The evaluators scanned this report but did not seriously consider its findings, since it was prepared while the program was still being developed. However, they decided to include the pilot test report in the appendix to their own report.

The evaluators subsequently implemented a test-retest of the participating students on the program's end-of-course test; periodic discussions of the program with groups of participating students, teachers, and administrators; annual interviews with teachers and curriculum specialists in each of the participating schools; and a cost analysis of the program. The evaluators presented their findings at the end of the two-year evaluation in a main report and an appendix. Their main report concentrated on the results of a repeated measures analysis of variance, controlled for type of district. This analysis produced the following results: pre-test—post-test gains were statistically significant at the .01 level for nine out of the twelve grades during the first year; corresponding gains were similarly statistically significant for all twelve grades during the second year; and the pattern of significance was similar for the three types of districts. Based on these findings, the main report concluded that the program was successful and recommended that it be widely disseminated.

Several staff members in the sponsoring agency criticized this field test report. They charged that the conclusion and recommendation were unjustified.

They pointed to results of the pilot test and to other information in the appendix that raised serious questions about the adequacy of the ecology program. This information suggested that the teachers—in both the pilot and field studies—taught the program's test but failed to implement planned activities; the school principals in both studies doubted that the program materials could be kept up to date at a reasonable cost; and the curriculum specialists were only lukewarm in their appraisal of the program. Based on the apparent disagreement between the main report and the appendix, the funding agency rejected the field test report.

**Analysis of the Case**  The evaluators who conducted the field test should have used all pertinent prior information about the program in formulating their conclusions and recommendations. Moreover, they should have developed their conclusions and recommendations to reflect all the findings of the field test—not just those based on student performance. Finally, they should not have claimed that the program was successful without providing adequate evidence to support the claim.

# D11 OBJECTIVE REPORTING

**Standard**    The evaluation procedures should provide safeguards to protect the evaluation findings and reports against distortion by the personal feelings and biases of any party to the evaluation.

**Overview**    Reports are objective to the extent that they are based on impartially assembled facts and are not slanted to promote biased positions. The former condition is difficult to meet. Human judgments enter into the selection of evaluation criteria and instruments, the choice of procedures for collecting and analyzing data, and the formulation of conclusions. Many of the preceding standards have dealt at least in part with responding to the problem of nonobjectivity in data collection and analysis (see A2, A4, B2, C2, C3, C7, D2, D4, D5, D6, and D10). This standard deals with the second condition, and seeks to provide guidance on how to develop and present reports in such ways that they will be as unbiased as possible and reveal any suspected biases to the audiences.

Reports can be rendered nonobjective in a variety of ways. In some cases the evaluator may fail to represent the many perspectives that should be taken into account, so that the report becomes biased because of an error of omission. In other cases the report is biased by an error of commission: the report is deliberately designed to deceive, to cover up, to whitewash, to confirm decisions already made on other grounds, and so on. Some distortions occur because of evaluators' ignorance or carelessness; others are introduced because of client/sponsor/audience pressure which the evaluator feels unable to resist. Bias can even be introduced as the direct result of the fact that reporting should be a continuous process, with frequent audience checks on information, validity, credibility, and so on. By virtue of such interaction the evaluator can become co-opted in ways that render subsequent reporting less objective.

**Guidelines**  A. Reach agreement with the client during the evaluation's initial stages about what steps will be taken to ensure that the reports will be honest and as objective as possible.

B. Ensure that the evaluation report will include perspectives that are independent from those of the staff whose work is being evaluated.

C. Seek out and report, to the fullest extent possible, conflicting points of view about what conclusions and recommendations are warranted.

D. Describe all steps taken in the evaluation to protect the integrity of the several reports, as well as the basis for those steps.

E. Seek out, examine, and report biases and prejudices which may have influenced the evaluation findings and conclusions in an unbalanced way, i.e., to a greater extent than they deserved.

F. Strive to establish and maintain evaluator independence in reporting, using techniques such as adversary-advocacy reports, outside audits, rotation of evaluation team members over various audience contacts, and the like.

**Pitfalls**  A. Assuming that all parties to an evaluation operate from a position of integrity that militates against deliberate efforts to obfuscate or deceive

B. Failing to consider the need to safeguard reports explicitly and to establish mechanisms to protect the reports against deliberate or inadvertent distortions

C. Surrendering the authority to edit reports

D. Failing to be involved in public oral presentations of the findings

**Caveats**  A. Do not establish so much independence from the group whose work is being evaluated that their ability to provide useful information to the evaluation is sacrificed or the evaluation's ability to provide useful feedback to them is largely diminished. Do recognize in the evaluation report, however, that these persons' involvement created opportunities for them to co-opt the evaluators; and, to offset the consequent possibility of bias, provide for independent examination of the reported findings and conclusions.

B. Do not become so engrossed in the protection of reports that chronic suspicion results, or that the evaluation becomes a witch-hunt instead of a calm, deliberate attempt to assess merit and worth.

**Illustrative Case**  A superintendent of a small school district decided to have a special reading project evaluated. The project had been introduced three years earlier within the early grades of one of the district's three elementary schools. It was now time for a decision about whether to institutionalize the project as the district's reading program. A reading specialist from a neighboring school district accepted the evaluation task.

As she began collecting data from and about children who had been exposed to the project, the evaluator formed the initial conclusion that the project was not successful and in fact was producing serious and undesirable side effects, particularly, she thought, destroying the motivation of children to read. She thought it wise to check this perception with the project staff, who, when she made a presentation to them, became very defensive and hostile. They suggested that her heavy reliance on test scores had seriously constrained her ability to really understand what the project was about. Moreover, they asserted, her own biases in favor of highly structured approaches to teaching reading, based on psychological theories of behavior modification, rendered her incompetent to judge the project's approach, which was based on more gestaltist points of view. The evaluator capitulated to the pressures brought to bear by the project staff and submitted a report to the superintendent recommending that the project be adopted as the reading program for the district.

**Analysis of the Case**  The evaluator, perhaps because of her inexperience, was too quick to submit to the criticism of a project staff that had an obvious axe to grind. Her reaction to their comments should not have been to capitulate but to test the extent to which the staff's observations were valid as opposed to being merely self-serving.

Other information could have been compiled to cross-check their assertion that test scores did not adequately represent project outcomes—an assertion that was probably true. She might have recognized the possibility that her own philosophical predilections about methods of teaching reading had influenced her judgment, and sought confirmation by employing—or at least consulting—other experts who could confirm or refute her own judgment. She should have realized that project staff would probably have developed an unreasoned commitment to what they were doing, and discounted their reactions accordingly. Finally, if the conflicts introduced by the staff's reactions could not have been resolved, she could have developed a final report that openly presented the conflicts, including her own value position, and noted their unresolved state. While not definitive, such a report would have reflected the true state of affairs to the superintendent with greater fidelity and would have avoided providing a warrant for a project whose effectiveness was very much in doubt.

# Appendix A

# DEVELOPMENT OF THE STANDARDS

The *Standards for Evaluations of Educational Programs, Projects, and Materials* evolved from the 1974 revision of the *Standards for Educational and Psychological Tests.*[1] The Joint Committee on Test Standards (JCTS) which accomplished that revision included representatives of the American Educational Research Association (AERA), the American Psychological Association (APA), and the National Council on Measurement in Education (NCME).

An early draft of the revised *Test Standards* contained a section on program evaluation and the use of tests in program evaluation. However, the JCTS expressed several reservations about including this section. First, the schedule for completing the *Test Standards* did not allow enough time to develop adequate standards for inclusion of the section. Second, the JCTS felt that many of the problems associated with evaluating group performance and curriculum and program efforts were beyond the scope of the document. Third, it believed that the complexity of the field of evaluation required more than one set of standards directed toward specific settings, i.e., education, social services, and public policy. Finally, it was concerned that the audiences for the two sets of standards were sufficiently different that the impact could better be targeted by separate documents. Faced with these concerns, the JCTS had to decide whether to begin a new draft which would include additional standards for program evaluation and interpretation of content-referenced test scores,

[1] American Psychological Association, *Standards for Educational and Psychological Tests* (Rev. Ed.) (Washington, D.C., APA, 1974).

or to delete this section from the draft and recommend the preparation of a companion volume of standards for program evaluation.

To help focus the deliberations, George Madaus, an NCME representative on the JCTS, prepared a May 7, 1973, memorandum making a strong case for a companion volume. On the basis of this memorandum, the JCTS deleted the section on program evaluation and interpretation of content-referenced test scores and recommended in the foreword of the *Test Standards* consideration of a companion volume focused on these topics.

Prompted by this recommendation, the APA Committee on Psychological Tests and Assessment explored the advisability of APA participating in a new project to develop standards for program evaluation and interpretation of content-referenced test scores. In the Spring of 1974 the APA Committee sent the Madaus memorandum, along with specific questions, to about 20 reviewers. The respondents generally agreed with Madaus' arguments and supported his proposal.

AERA and NCME also considered participating in an evaluation standards project. They reviewed pertinent documents and discussed them at their board meetings. NCME also surveyed its membership and found that program evaluation was given the highest priority for attention by NCME.[2]

Based on Madaus' conceptual leadership, the favorable evaluations of his proposal, and the recognized need to improve program evaluation, AERA, APA, and NCME appointed the initial Joint Committee on Standards for Educational Evaluation (Joint Committee) and charged them to prepare a proposal outlining the appropriate objectives, procedures, schedule, and budget for implementing such a project. The Committee included:

AERA representative:
Egon Guba

---

[2] "A Profile of NCME Members," NCME *Measurement News*, 18(4), October, 1974.

APA representatives:
Donald Campbell
Robert Linn
Henry Riecken

NCME representatives:
Ron Carver
George Madaus
Daniel Stufflebeam

In May, 1975, members of this group met in Chicago. They reviewed the emerging field of evaluation, and agreed that guidelines and standards for evaluation should be developed; but they decided that the focus of such an effort should be broadened beyond the specific issue concerning the use of tests in evaluation. They concluded, however, that their initial effort should concentrate on evaluation in education as opposed to other fields. They also agreed that the Joint Committee should be expanded to represent the various groups involved in evaluating education.

Based on these decisions, the initial Joint Committee agreed on the following mission statement:

The goal of the Joint Committee will be to develop guidelines and possibly standards for evaluation in educational settings. The central focus will be on problems in evaluating educational programs, projects, and materials.

The Committee also developed a set of objectives and a set of policies to govern the project. These evolved during the course of the project, and a complete history of how the objectives and policies changed during the project is in the public file in the Evaluation Center at Western Michigan University.

The policy that proved to be most influential in the developmental process was the one calling for a committee with broad representation. Approximately, this committee was to have 18 members, including nine that represent groups oriented toward improving evaluation methodology and nine that represent groups oriented toward improving the application of evaluation methodology.

After developing the first draft of the mission statement, objectives, and policies, the initial Joint Committee concluded its May, 1975 meeting by deciding to carry out a series of next steps. These included drafting a proposal, recruiting selected agencies to membership in the Evaluation Standards venture, and organizing a 1975 Fall meeting of the expanded Joint Committee.

These actions were taken and the expanded Joint Committee convened in Chicago on December 3, 1975. This group received, modified, and approved the draft proposal, discussed many issues related to the project, decided on an additional expansion of the Joint Committee, elected Dr. Stufflebeam to be Chairman of the Committee, and directed him to search for financial support for the project.

Following this meeting, a first-year grant was obtained from the Lilly Endowment. Funds for the remainder of the project were later received from the National Institute of Education, the National Science Foundation, and the Weyerhaeuser Company Foundation, as well as the sponsoring organizations.

Beginning in April, 1976, the funded project got underway. The Joint Committee in cooperation with the Project Staff, located at the Western Michigan University Evaluation Center, identified four categories of standards, (Utility, Feasibility, Propriety, and Accuracy), and developed a list of topics for each category (e.g., Report Timeliness, Cost Effectiveness, Full and Frank Disclosure, and Reliable Measurement). They also devised a set of guidelines for converting each topic into a fully described standard. They then recruited a nationwide panel of experts in various aspects of evaluation and commissioned each member to write several standards. After this charge was fulfilled, the Joint Committee and the Project Staff met in Chicago in December of 1976 to critique and rewrite the standards. Following the meeting, the Project Staff, a graduate seminar at Western Michigan University, and a subcommittee of the Joint Committee compiled the standards into the first draft of this book.

This draft version of the *Standards* was sent out for review in July of 1977 to the National Review Panel, whose members had been nominated by the members of the Joint Committee. The Project

Staff compiled the reactions that were obtained and then met with the Joint Committee in October of 1977 to plan the revision of the first draft of the *Standards*. They also reviewed the first draft of a condensed version of the *Standards* that had been prepared by the Project Staff and the Committee.

Following the Fall, 1977 meeting, the Project Staff and the Joint Committee revised the full-length and condensed forms of the *Standards*, and they obtained reviews of the condensed form from a panel of about fifty persons who had been appointed by the twelve sponsoring organizations. At their Fall, 1978 meeting, the Committee studied the results from the review of the condensed form and tabled any further work on this form. This decision reflected the Committee's conclusion that the condensed form could not be developed further until the full length form had been finalized; some members also noted that a condensed form might not be needed if the full-length version was shortened in the final editing process. The Committee also developed specifications for a revision of the long form and approved plans for national hearings and a field test of this form.

The first half of 1979 was devoted to field tests and public hearings on the long form of the *Standards*; and many detailed critiques were obtained. Also, a panel of distinguished representatives of various disciplines outside education was invited to evaluate the adequacy of the *Standards* from their various perspectives; but few responses were received. Next, the long form was revised based on the results of the field tests, the hearings, and the expert reviews. The Project Staff and the Joint Committee met in the Fall of 1979 to finalize the long form, based on the critiques they had obtained. They reconsidered the issues of the condensed form and again decided to table any further work on that form. Subsequently, the Project Staff completed the long form and submitted it for publication in 1980.

The complete historical documentation of the project is on file at the Evaluation Center, Western Michigan University. This file includes all standards that were considered and all reports and documents that were developed in relation to the project.

# Appendix B

# CITING THE STANDARDS

Evaluators may wish to cite the use of the *Standards* as guiding an evaluation proposal, plan, contract, request, or audit. References to the use of the *Standards* should not be made unless accompanied by statements of the extent to which the individual standards were considered.

The Joint Committee has developed a citation form which covers different levels of use and/or consideration of the *Standards*. This form is reproduced on the following page and provides a range of options for indicating the extent to which each standard was considered. It should be noted that in many evaluations (especially low budget formative evaluations), systematic application and documentation of the *Standards* will not be feasible; nevertheless, use of the form is recommended, and permission for users to reproduce the form is hereby given. The form should be completed, signed and placed inside the back cover of the evaluation proposal, plan, contract, request, or audit.

The Joint Committee, in order to facilitate its ongoing review of the *Standards*, would also appreciate receiving a copy of the completed form; it should be sent to

Joint Committee on Standards for Educational Evaluation
% The Evaluation Center
Western Michigan University
Kalamazoo, Michigan 49008

(616)383-8166

# APPENDIX                                          B

**Citation Form***

The *Standards for Evaluations of Educational Programs, Projects, and Materials* guided the development of this (check one):

    request for evaluation plan/design/proposal
    evaluation plan/design/proposal
    evaluation contract
    evaluation report
    other

**To interpret the information provided on this form, the reader needs to refer to the full text of the standards as they appear in** Joint Committee on Standards for Educational Evaluation, *Standards for Evaluations of Educational Programs, Projects, and Materials.* New York: McGraw-Hill, 1980

The *Standards* were consulted and used as indicated in the table below (check as appropriate):

| Descriptor | | The Standard was deemed applicable and to the extent feasible was taken into account | The Standard was deemed applicable but could not be taken into account | The Standard was not deemed applicable | Exception was taken to the Standard |
|---|---|---|---|---|---|
| A1 | Audience Identification | | | | |
| A2 | Evaluator Credibility | | | | |
| A3 | Information Scope and Selection | | | | |
| A4 | Valuational Interpretation | | | | |
| A5 | Report Clarity | | | | |
| A6 | Report Dissemination | | | | |
| A7 | Report Timeliness | | | | |
| A8 | Evaluation Impact | | | | |
| B1 | Practical Procedures | | | | |
| B2 | Political Viability | | | | |
| B3 | Cost Effectiveness | | | | |
| C1 | Formal Obligation | | | | |
| C2 | Conflict of Interest | | | | |
| C3 | Full and Frank Disclosure | | | | |
| C4 | Public's Right to Know | | | | |
| C5 | Rights of Human Subjects | | | | |
| C6 | Human Interactions | | | | |
| C7 | Balanced Reporting | | | | |
| C8 | Fiscal Responsibility | | | | |
| D1 | Object Identification | | | | |
| D2 | Context Analysis | | | | |
| D3 | Described Purposes and Procedures | | | | |
| D4 | Defensible Information Sources | | | | |
| D5 | Valid Measurement | | | | |
| D6 | Reliable Measurement | | | | |
| D7 | Systematic Data Control | | | | |
| D8 | Analysis of Quantitative Information | | | | |
| D9 | Analysis of Qualitative Information | | | | |
| D10 | Justified Conclusions | | | | |
| D11 | Objective Reporting | | | | |

Name: _____ Date: _____
        (typed)

_____
        (signature)

Position or Title: _____

Agency: _____

Address: _____

Relation to Document: _____
        (e.g., author of document, evaluation team leader, external auditor, internal auditor)

*The Publisher gives permission to photocopy this form.

# GLOSSARY

Terms are defined in this glossary mainly as they are used in this volume, in the context of evaluation. In other contexts, a number of the terms may have broader or different definitions.

**Accuracy** — The extent to which an evaluation is truthful or valid in what it says about a program, project, or material.

**Adversarial/advocacy "group"** — A group of people who enter into cross-examination of counter plans, strategies, or outcomes.

**Advocacy teams** — Groups of people who are brought together to develop competing strategies for achieving a given set of objectives.

**Affective dimension** — The psychological concept that refers to a person's feelings, emotions, or degree of acceptance or rejection of some object.

**Analysis of covariance** — A technique for analyzing data often used to make a decision about whether differences occurred by chance.

**Analysis of variance** — A method for determining whether the differences between groups are statistically significant.

**Anonymity (provision for)** — Evaluator action to ensure that the identity of subjects cannot be ascertained during the course of a study or in study reports.

**Archival search** — An examination of existing records, reports, and documents pertaining to the object of the evaluation.

**Assessment** — The act of determining the standing of an object on some variable of interest. For example, testing students and reporting raw scores.

**Attrition** — Loss of subjects from the defined sample during the course of a study.

**Audiences** — Those persons who will be guided by the evaluation in making decisions and all others who have a stake in the evaluation.

**Audit (of an evaluation)** — An independent examination and verification of the quality of an evaluation plan, the adequacy with which it was implemented, the accuracy of results, and the validity of conclusions.

**Bias** — A consistent alignment with one point of view.

**Case study** — An intensive, detailed description and analysis of a single project, program, or instructional material in the context of its environment.

**Caveat** — A discussion of the tradeoffs that may be necessary in applying the standard. These are mistakes based on being overzealous in the application of the standard.

| | |
|---|---|
| Client | The individual, group, or organization which hires the evaluator. |
| Code (information) | To translate a given set of data or items into a set of quantitative or qualitative symbols. |
| Coefficient | A value expressing the degree to which some characteristic or relation is to be found in specified instances; e.g., the coefficient of correlation is a value expressing the degree to which two variables vary concomitantly. |
| Cognitive ability | The psychological concept that refers to such processes as perceiving, knowing, recognizing, conceptualizing, judging, and reasoning. |
| Comparative experimental studies | Studies that assign a program, project, or instructional material to one group of persons and compare their subsequent performance on some structured task to that of another group that was not exposed to the program, project, or instructional material. |
| Comparison group (in experimentation) | A group which provides a basis for contrast with an experimental group (i.e., the group of people participating in the program or project being evaluated). The comparison group is not subjected to the treatment (independent variable), thus creating a means for comparison with the experimental group, which does receive the treatment. |
| Conclusions (of an evaluation) | Final judgments and recommendations. |
| Conditioning | Associating a response with a previously unrelated stimulus through repeated presentation of the stimulus to a subject at the same time (or almost the same time) with another stimulus normally yielding the response. |
| Content analysis | The process of identifying and listing—in accordance with a parsimonious classification system—the ideas, feelings, personal references, and other categories of expression contained in a variety of information sources. |
| Context (of an evaluation) | The combination of the factors accompanying the study that may have influenced its results. These factors include the geographic location of the study, its timing, the political and social climate in the region at that time, the other relevant professional activities that were in progress, and any existing pertinent economic conditions. |
| Contract | A written or oral agreement between the evaluator and the client which is enforceable by law. It is a mutual understanding of expectations and responsibilities for both parties. |
| Control group | A group as closely as possible equivalent to an experimental group (one that is exposed to a program, project, or instructional material), and exposed to all the conditions of the investigation except the program, project, or instructional material being studied. |
| Convergence group | A group which is responsible for incorporating the important features of alternative strategies proposed by advocacy teams into a compromise strategy. |
| Correlation | A statistical measure of the degree of relationship between or among variables. It is expressed in the form of an index that may vary from $-1.00$ to $+1.00$. |

**Cost effectiveness** The extent to which one program, project, or instructional material produces equal or better results than competitors that cost about the same amount of time, effort, and resources; or the extent to which an object produces the same results as competitors but is less costly.

**Covariate** A variate occurring concomitantly with the variate of primary interest and measured for the purpose of making informed adjustments on the variate of primary interest (e.g., measuring pretest performance of two groups in order to adjust their posttest scores so that they take account of differences between groups that existed prior to the treatment of one of the groups).

**Criterion** A standard by which something can be judged.

**Criterion-referenced tests** Tests whose scores are interpreted by referral to specifically defined performances, rather than by referral to the performance of some comparable group of people.

**Data** Material gathered during the course of an evaluation which serves as the basis for information, discussion, and inference.

**Data access** The extent to which the evaluator will be permitted to obtain data during the course of an evaluation.

**Decision rule** A rule for choosing between optional interpretations or courses of action given certain evidence (e.g., a rule by which teachers pass or fail students in a course based on their test scores and other performances in the course; a rule by which a government agency ranks project proposals for funding based on their contents and the ratings assigned to them by judges; or a rule by which an evaluator decides that the difference between the test scores of students exposed to different programs is statistically significant).

**Delphi Technique** A method for obtaining group consensus involving the use of a series of mailed questionnaires and controlled feedback to respondents which continues until consensus is reached.

**Dependent variable** A measure (e.g., a student's performance on a test) that is assumed to vary as a result of some influence (often taken to be the independent variable), such as a student's instructional experience.

**Design (evaluation)** A representation of the set of decisions that determine how an evaluation is to be conducted; e.g., data collection schedule, report schedules, questions to be addressed, analysis plan, management plan, etc. Designs may be either preordinate or emergent.

**Dissemination** The communication of the actions—by written, oral, and/or audio-visual reporting—of evaluators to foster knowledge of the evaluation findings among all right-to-know audiences.

**Editorial authority** The extent of the evaluator's authority to edit evaluation reports prior to dissemination.

**Emergent design** An implementation plan in which the specification of every step depends upon the results of previous steps, sometimes also known as a cascading or rolling design.

**Escrow agent** A third party that, by agreement, controls certain information, such as the names on tests, submitted by a first party, so that this information is not obtained by the second party.

**Evaluation** Systematic investigation of the worth or merit of an object; e.g., a program, project, or instructional material.

**Evaluator** Anyone who accepts and executes responsibility for planning, conducting, and reporting evaluations.

**Executive report** An abbreviated report that has been tailored specifically to address the concerns and questions of a person whose function is to administer an educational program or project.

**Executive summary** A summary statement designed to provide a quick overview of the full-length report on which it is based.

**Experimental design** The plan of an experiment, including selection of subjects, order of administration of the experimental treatment, the kind of treatment, the procedures by which it is administered, and the recording of the data (with special reference to the particular statistical analyses to be performed).

**Experimental group** A group of subjects assigned to receive a treatment (independent variable) the effects of which are measured (dependent variable). Often comparisons are made between these effects and those observed for a comparison (nontreatment) group.

**Experimental research** Scientific investigation in which an investigator manipulates and controls one or more independent variables to determine their effects on the outcome (dependent) variable.

**External evaluation** Evaluation conducted by an evaluator from outside the organization within which the object of the study is housed.

**Extrapolate** To infer an unknown from something that is known. (Statistical definition—to estimate the value of a variable outside its observed range.)

**Feasibility** The extent to which an evaluation is appropriate for implementation in practical settings.

**Field test** The study of a program, project, or instructional material in a setting like those where it is to be used. Field tests may range from preliminary primative investigations to full-scale summative studies.

**Formative evaluation** Evaluation designed and used to improve an object, especially when it is still being developed.

**Gain scores** The difference between a student's performance on a test and his or her performance on a subsequent administration of the same test.

**Generalizability** The extent to which information about a program, project, or instructional material collected in one setting can be used to reach a valid judgment about how it will perform in other settings.

**Generic rights** Rights that are shared by all members of a group.

**Goal-free evaluation** Evaluation of outcomes in which the evaluator functions without knowledge of the purposes or goals.

**Guideline** A procedural suggestion intended to help evaluators and their audiences to meet the requirements of the evaluation standards; strategy to avoid mistakes in applying the standards.

**Hardware (data processing)** The physical components, such as a computer and keypunch machine, of a data processing system, as opposed to the instructional (content-related) components.

**Illustrative case** An illustration of how a standard might be applied, which includes the description of a certain setting, a situation in which the standard is not met, and a discussion of corrective actions that would result in the standard being met.

**Information needs** Information requirements of the evaluator, clients, and other pertinent audiences to be met by the evaluation.

**Information sources** The persons, groups, and documents from which data are obtained.

**Informed consent** Agreement by the participants in an evaluation to the use of their names and/or confidential information supplied by them in specified ways, for stated purposes, and in light of possible consequences prior to the collection and/or release of this information in evaluation reports.

**Instrument** An assessment device adopted, adapted, or constructed for the purposes of the evaluation.

**Internal evaluation** Evaluation conducted by a staff member from within the organization being studied.

**Jury trial for projects** Project evaluations patterned after jury trials in their procedures for clarifying issues, introducing and assessing evidence, and reaching conclusions. Sometimes known as Adversary Model of evaluation.

**Level of significance** A predetermined probability value used to decide whether the results occurred by chance.

**Matching** An experimental procedure in which the subjects are so divided, by means other than lottery, that the groups are regarded for the purposes at hand to be of equal merit or ability. (Often matched groups are created by ensuring that they are the same or nearly so on such variables as sex, age, grade point averages, and past test scores.)

**Materials evaluation** Evaluations that assess the merit or worth of content-related physical items, including books, curricular guides, films, tapes, and other tangible instructional products.

**Mean (arithmetic)** A measure of central tendency calculated by dividing the sum of all the values by the number of the values.

**Merit** The excellence of an object as assessed by its intrinsic qualities or performance.

**Meta evaluation** Evaluation of an evaluation.

**Modus operandi analysis** Deducing the cause of effects based upon analysis of events, process, or properties associated with the effects; analogous to procedures used in detective work.

| | |
|---|---|
| **"No significant difference"** | A label reflecting a decision that an observed difference between two statistics occurred by chance. |
| **Norm** | A single value, or a distribution of values, constituting the typical performance of a given group. |
| **Null hypothesis** | The hypothesis of no difference or no effects. |
| **Object of the evaluation** | What one is evaluating; e.g., a program, a project, or instructional material. |
| **Objectives-referenced test** | A test whose scores are referenced to the attainment of the objectives the test was designed to measure, rather than the performance on the test by some comparison group of people. |
| **Operational definition** | A definition of a term or object achieved by stating the operations or procedures employed to distinguish it from others. |
| **Overview** | A conceptual/introductory statement that gives essential definitions; provides a general rationale; and presents summarized procedures, common problems, and special difficulties that are applicable. An explication of the standard. |
| **Parallel forms** | Multiple forms of a test constructed to be as comparable and interchangeable as possible in their content, length, and procedures of administration, and in the scores and test properties (e.g., means, variances, and reliability indices). |
| **Pilot test** | A brief and simplified preliminary study designed to try out methods to learn whether a proposed project or program seems likely to yield valuable results. |
| **Pitfall** | A not easily recognized difficulty believed to be associated with a particular standard. These are mistakes that would be made out of ignorance of the import and intent of a standard. |
| **Population** | All the persons in the group to which conclusions from a study are to be applied. |
| **Post-test** | A test to determine performance after the administration of a program, project, or instructional material. |
| **Pre-test** | A test to determine performance prior to the administration of a program, project, or instructional material. |
| **Program evaluations** | Evaluations that assess educational activities which provide services on a continuing basis and often involve curricular offerings. Examples include evaluation of a school district's reading program, a state's special education program, and a university's continuing education program. |
| **Project evaluations** | Evaluations that assess activities that are funded for a defined period of time to perform a specified task. Some examples are a three-day workshop on behavioral objectives, a two-year development effort, or a three-year career education demonstration. |
| **Propriety** | The extent to which the evaluation has been conducted in a manner that evidences uncompromising adherence to the highest principles and ideals (including professional ethics, civil law, moral code, and contractual agreements). |

| | |
|---|---|
| **Purposes (of an evaluation study)** | The objectives of an evaluation (e.g., to judge the relative merits of competing textbooks, or to monitor and report on how well a project plan is implemented) and the intended uses of its reports (e.g., to help teachers choose a textbook or to help a school district carry out a special project). |
| **Qualitative information** | Facts and claims presented in narrative, not numerical, form. |
| **Quantitative information** | Facts and claims that are represented by numbers. |
| **Random** | Occurring by chance. |
| **Random sampling** | Drawing a number of items of any sort from a larger group or population so that every individual item has the same (an independent) chance as any other to be chosen. |
| **Regression to the mean** | The tendency of scores of examinees above or below the mean of a distribution on a pretest to score closer to the mean on the posttest. |
| **Reinforce** | To strengthen a learned way of behaving by some external or internal influence. |
| **Reliable measure** | A measure that provides consistent indications of the characteristics being measured. |
| **Replicate** | To repeat an evaluation with all essentials unchanged. |
| **Right-to-know audience** | A group of people entitled to be informed about the results of the evaluation. |
| **Sample** | A part of a population. |
| **School profile** | A description (graphic, numeric, or variable) of the status of a school with respect to a set of concepts or variables. |
| **Secondary data analysis** | A reanalysis of data using the same or other appropriate procedures to verify the accuracy of the results of the initial analysis or for answering different questions. |
| **Self-report instrument** | A device in which persons make and report judgments about the functioning of their project, program, or instructional material. |
| **"Significant difference" (statistically)** | A label reflecting a decision that an observed difference between two statistics did not occur by chance. |
| **Simulation study** | A study in which the probable effects of alternative solutions to a problem are identified by using symbolic representations of real activities, situations, or environments. |
| **Sociodrama** | Dramatization and role playing used to teach an audience about the findings of an evaluation and to illustrate their potential applications. |
| **Sponsor** | The individual, group, or organization which provides the funds for the evaluation. |
| **Standard** | A principle commonly agreed to by experts in the conduct and use of evaluation for the measure of the value or quality of an evaluation. |
| **Standardized test** | A sample of items or situations with definite directions for administration and scoring most often accomplished by data on reliability and validity and sometimes by normative information. |

| | |
|---|---|
| Statistic | A summary number that is typically used to describe a characteristic of a sample. |
| Stratified random sample | A grouping achieved by dividing the population to be surveyed into a number of nonoverlapping classes or categories which together include all cases, followed by taking cases at random from within the categories, the number from each category being proportional to the total number therein. |
| Summative evaluation | Evaluation designed to present conclusions about the merit or worth of an object and recommendations about whether it should be retained, altered, or eliminated. |
| System analysis | The discovery and identification of sources of error or variability in a system, the measurement of these errors, and the arrangement of system elements to improve system performance. |
| Terminal | A device connected to a computer by telephone lines that permits use of the computer at locations physically separated from the computer. |
| Test retest reliability | The extent to which two administrations of the same test to the same group of subjects yield consistent results. |
| Time series study | A study in which periodic measurements are obtained prior to and following the introduction of an intervention or treatment in order to reach conclusions about the effect of the intervention. |
| Unit of analysis | A single thing, person, or group that is a constituent and isolable member of some more inclusive whole; a member of an aggregate that is the least part to have clearly definable separate existence and that normally forms a basic element of organization within the aggregate; the least divisible element on which measures are taken and analyzed. |
| Utility | The extent to which an evaluation produces and disseminates reports that inform relevant audiences and have beneficial impact on their work. |
| Validity | The soundness of the use and interpretation of a measure. |
| Values clarification techniques | Procedures used to help groups recognize the different values held in the groups, to discern conflicts among these values, and to consider how these conflicts might be resolved. |
| Variable | A characteristic that can take on different values. |
| Variate | The quantitative measure of a variable. |
| Word attack skills | Means by which a person recognizes and perceives the meaning of a word. |
| Worth | The value of an object in relationship to a purpose. |

# INDEX

# FEEDBACK FORM

The Joint Committee, in an effort to obtain feedback on the *Standards*, has provided the attached feedback form for the reader's convenience. Detach and return the form for: (1) information regarding the review process for the *Standards*; (2) a supply of feedback and citation forms; and (3) directions regarding the use of the forms. Please refer to Invitation to Users for an overview of the plan for reviewing and improving the *Standards*.

General inquiries concerning the *Standards* should be directed to:

Joint Committee on Standards for Educational Evaluation
c/o The Evaluation Center
Western Michigan University
Kalamazoo, Michigan 49008
(616) 383-8166

Please send review process information and a supply of feedback and citation forms, and directions for the use of the forms to:

_____

Name

_____

_____

Institution